HOLT
SCIENCE &
TECHNOLOGY

Interactions
of Matter

HOLT, RINEHART AND WINSTON

A Harcourt Classroom Education Company

Austin · New York · Orlando · Atlanta · San Francisco · Boston · Dallas · Toronto · London

Staff Credits

Editorial

Robert W. Todd, Executive Editor

Anne Earvolino, Senior Editor

Michael Mazza, Ken Shepardson, Kelly Rizk, Bill Burnside, Editors

ANCILLARIES

Jennifer Childers, Senior Editor

Chris Colby, Molly Frohlich, Shari Husain, Kristen McCardel, Sabelyn Pussman, Erin Roberson

COPYEDITING

Dawn Spinozza, Copyediting Supervisor

EDITORIAL SUPPORT STAFF

Jeanne Graham, Mary Helbling, Tanu'e White, Doug Rutley

EDITORIAL PERMISSIONS

Cathy Paré, Permissions Manager

Jan Harrington, Permissions Editor

Art, Design, and Photo

BOOK DESIGN

Richard Metzger, Design Director

Marc Cooper, Senior Designer

Ron Bowdoin, Designer

Alicia Sullivan, Designer (ATE), **Cristina Bowerman,** Design Associate (ATE)

Eric Rupprath, Designer (Ancillaries)

Holly Whittaker, Traffic Coordinator

IMAGE ACQUISITIONS

Joe London, Director

Elaine Tate, Art Buyer Supervisor

Tim Taylor, Photo Research Supervisor

Stephanie Morris, Assistant Photo Researcher

PHOTO STUDIO

Sam Dudgeon, Senior Staff Photographer

Victoria Smith, Photo Specialist

Lauren Eischen, Photo Coordinator

DESIGN NEW MEDIA

Susan Michael, Design Director

Production

Mimi Stockdell, Senior Production Manager

Beth Sample, Senior Production Coordinator

Suzanne Brooks, Sara Carroll-Downs

Media Production

Kim A. Scott, Senior Production Manager

Adriana Bardin-Prestwood, Senior Production Coordinator

New Media

Armin Gutzmer, Director

Jim Bruno, Senior Project Manager

Lydia Doty, Senior Project Manager

Jessica Bega, Project Manager

Cathy Kuhles, Nina Degollado, Technical Assistants

Design Implementation and Production

The Quarasan Group, Inc.

Acknowledgments

Chapter Writers

Christie Borgford, Ph.D.
Professor of Chemistry
University of Alabama
Birmingham, Alabama

Andrew Champagne
Former Physics Teacher
Ashland High School
Ashland, Massachusetts

Mapi Cuevas, Ph.D.
Professor of Chemistry
Santa Fe Community College
Gainesville, Florida

Leila Dumas
Former Physics Teacher
LBJ Science Academy
Austin, Texas

William G. Lamb, Ph.D.
Science Teacher and Dept. Chair
Oregon Episcopal School
Portland, Oregon

Sally Ann Vonderbrink, Ph.D.
Chemistry Teacher
St. Xavier High School
Cincinnati, Ohio

Lab Writers

Phillip G. Bunce
Former Physics Teacher
Bowie High School
Austin, Texas

Kenneth E. Creese
Science Teacher
White Mountain Junior High School
Rock Springs, Wyoming

William G. Lamb, Ph.D.
Science Teacher and Dept. Chair
Oregon Episcopal School
Portland, Oregon

Alyson Mike
Science Teacher
East Valley Middle School
East Helena, Montana

Joseph W. Price
Science Teacher and Dept. Chair
H. M. Browne Junior High School
Washington, D.C.

Denice Lee Sandefur
Science Teacher and Dept. Chair
Nucla High School
Nucla, Colorado

John Spadafino
Mathematics and Physics Teacher
Hackensack High School
Hackensack, New Jersey

Walter Woolbaugh
Science Teacher
Manhattan Junior High School
Manhattan, Montana

Academic Reviewers

Paul R. Berman, Ph.D.
Professor of Physics
University of Michigan
Ann Arbor, Michigan

Russell M. Brengelman, Ph.D.
Professor of Physics
Morehead State University
Morehead, Kentucky

John A. Brockhaus, Ph.D.
Director, Mapping, Charting and Geodesy Program
Department of Geography and Environmental Engineering
United States Military Academy
West Point, New York

Walter Bron, Ph.D.
Professor of Physics
University of California
Irvine, California

Andrew J. Davis, Ph.D.
Manager, ACE Science Center
Department of Physics
California Institute of Technology
Pasadena, California

Peter E. Demmin, Ed.D.
Former Science Teacher and Department Chair
Amherst Central High School
Amherst, New York

Roger Falcone, Ph.D.
Professor of Physics and Department Chair
University of California
Berkeley, California

Cassandra A. Fraser, Ph.D.
Assistant Professor of Chemistry
University of Virginia
Charlottesville, Virginia

L. John Gagliardi, Ph.D.
Associate Professor of Physics and Department Chair
Rutgers University
Camden, New Jersey

Gabriele F. Giuliani, Ph.D.
Professor of Physics
Purdue University
West Lafayette, Indiana

Roy W. Hann, Jr., Ph.D.
Professor of Civil Engineering
Texas A&M University
College Station, Texas

John L. Hubisz, Ph.D.
Professor of Physics
North Carolina State University
Raleigh, North Carolina

Samuel P. Kounaves, Ph.D.
Professor of Chemistry
Tufts University
Medford, Massachusetts

Karol Lang, Ph.D.
Associate Professor of Physics
The University of Texas
Austin, Texas

Gloria Langer, Ph.D.
Professor of Physics
University of Colorado
Boulder, Colorado

Phillip LaRoe
Professor
Helena College of Technology
Helena, Montana

Joseph A. McClure, Ph.D.
Associate Professor of Physics
Georgetown University
Washington, D.C.

LaMoine L. Motz, Ph.D.
Coordinator of Science Education
Department of Learning Services
Oakland County Schools
Waterford, Michigan

R. Thomas Myers, Ph.D.
Professor of Chemistry, Emeritus
Kent State University
Kent, Ohio

Hillary Clement Olson, Ph.D.
Research Associate
Institute for Geophysics
The University of Texas
Austin, Texas

David P. Richardson, Ph.D.
Professor of Chemistry
Thompson Chemical Laboratory
Williams College
Williamstown, Massachusetts

John Rigden, Ph.D.
Director of Special Projects
American Institute of Physics
Colchester, Vermont

Peter Sheridan, Ph.D.
Professor of Chemistry
Colgate University
Hamilton, New York

Vederaman Sriraman, Ph.D.
Associate Professor of Technology
Southwest Texas State University
San Marcos, Texas

Jack B. Swift, Ph.D.
Professor of Physics
The University of Texas
Austin, Texas

Atiq Syed, Ph.D.
Master Instructor of Mathematics and Science
Texas State Technical College
Harlingen, Texas

Leonard Taylor, Ph.D.
Professor Emeritus
Department of Electrical Engineering
University of Maryland
College Park, Maryland

Virginia L. Trimble, Ph.D.
Professor of Physics and Astronomy
University of California
Irvine, California

Acknowledgments (cont.)

Martin VanDyke, Ph.D.
Professor of Chemistry, Emeritus
Front Range Community
    College
Westminster, Colorado

Gabriela Waschewsky, Ph.D.
Science and Math Teacher
Emery High School
Emeryville, California

Safety Reviewer

Jack A. Gerlovich, Ph.D.
Associate Professor
School of Education
Drake University
Des Moines, Iowa

Teacher Reviewers

Barry L. Bishop
Science Teacher and Dept. Chair
San Rafael Junior High School
Ferron, Utah

Paul Boyle
Science Teacher
Perry Heights Middle School
Evansville, Indiana

Kenneth Creese
Science Teacher
White Mountain Junior High
    School
Rock Springs, Wyoming

Vicky Farland
Science Teacher and Dept. Chair
Centennial Middle School
Yuma, Arizona

Rebecca Ferguson
Science Teacher
North Ridge Middle School
North Richland Hills, Texas

Laura Fleet
Science Teacher
Alice B. Landrum Middle
    School
Ponte Vedra Beach, Florida

Jennifer Ford
Science Teacher and Dept. Chair
North Ridge Middle School
North Richland Hills, Texas

Susan Gorman
Science Teacher
North Ridge Middle School
North Richland Hills, Texas

C. John Graves
Science Teacher
Monforton Middle School
Bozeman, Montana

Dennis Hanson
Science Teacher and Dept. Chair
Big Bear Middle School
Big Bear Lake, California

David A. Harris
Science Teacher and Dept. Chair
The Thacher School
Ojai, California

Norman E. Holcomb
Science Teacher
Marion Local Schools
Maria Stein, Ohio

Kenneth J. Horn
Science Teacher and Dept. Chair
Fallston Middle School
Fallston, Maryland

Tracy Jahn
Science Teacher
Berkshire Junior-Senior High
    School
Canaan, New York

Kerry A. Johnson
Science Teacher
Isbell Middle School
Santa Paula, California

Drew E. Kirian
Science Teacher
Solon Middle School
Solon, Ohio

Harriet Knops
Science Teacher and Dept. Chair
Rolling Hills Middle School
El Dorado, California

Scott Mandel, Ph.D.
*Director and Educational
    Consultant*
Teachers Helping Teachers
Los Angeles, California

Thomas Manerchia
Former Science Teacher
Archmere Academy
Claymont, Delaware

Edith McAlanis
Science Teacher and Dept. Chair
Socorro Middle School
El Paso, Texas

Kevin McCurdy, Ph.D.
Science Teacher
Elmwood Junior High School
Rogers, Arkansas

Alyson Mike
Science Teacher
East Valley Middle School
East Helena, Montana

Donna Norwood
Science Teacher and Dept. Chair
Monroe Middle School
Charlotte, North Carolina

Joseph W. Price
Science Teacher and Dept. Chair
H. M. Browne Junior High
    School
Washington, D.C.

Terry J. Rakes
Science Teacher
Elmwood Junior High School
Rogers, Arkansas

Beth Richards
Science Teacher
North Middle School
Crystal Lake, Illinois

Elizabeth J. Rustad
Science Teacher
Crane Middle School
Yuma, Arizona

Rodney A. Sandefur
Science Teacher
Naturita Middle School
Naturita, Colorado

Helen Schiller
Science Teacher
Northwood Middle School
Taylors, South Carolina

Bert J. Sherwood
Science Teacher
Socorro Middle School
El Paso, Texas

Patricia McFarlane Soto
Science Teacher and Dept. Chair
G. W. Carver Middle School
Miami, Florida

David M. Sparks
Science Teacher
Redwater Junior High School
Redwater, Texas

Larry Tackett
Science Teacher and Dept. Chair
Andrew Jackson Middle School
Cross Lanes, West Virginia

Elsie N. Waynes
Science Teacher and Dept. Chair
R. H. Terrell Junior High School
Washington, D.C.

Sharon L. Woolf
Science Teacher
Langston Hughes Middle
    School
Reston, Virginia

Alexis S. Wright
*Middle School Science
    Coordinator*
Rye Country Day School
Rye, New York

Lee Yassinski
Science Teacher
Sun Valley Middle School
Sun Valley, California

John Zambo
Science Teacher
Elizabeth Ustach Middle School
Modesto, California

Interactions of Matter

Skills Development

Connections

To the Student

This book was created to make your science experience interesting, exciting, and fun!

Go for It!

Science is a process of discovery, a trek into the unknown. The skills you develop using *Holt Science & Technology*— such as observing, experimenting, and explaining observations and ideas— are the skills you will need for the future. There is a universe of exploration and discovery awaiting those who accept the challenges of science.

Science & Technology

You see the interaction between science and technology every day. Science makes technology possible. On the other hand, some of the products of technology, such as computers, are used to make further scientific discoveries. In fact, much of the scientific work that is done today has become so technically complicated and expensive that no one person can do it entirely alone. But make no mistake, the creative ideas for even the most highly technical and expensive scientific work still come from individuals.

Activities and Labs

The activities and labs in this book will allow you to make some basic but important scientific discoveries on your own. You can even do some exploring on your own at home! Here's your chance to use your imagination and curiosity as you investigate your world.

Keep a ScienceLog

In this book, you will be asked to keep a type of journal called a ScienceLog to record your thoughts, observations, experiments, and conclusions. As you develop your ScienceLog, you will see your own ideas taking shape over time. You'll have a written record of how your ideas have changed as you learn about and explore interesting topics in science.

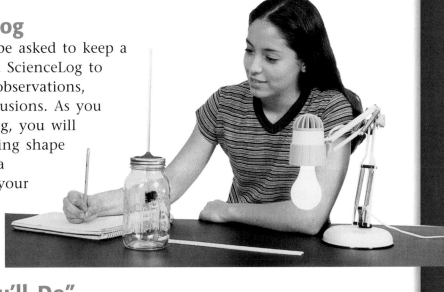

Know "What You'll Do"

The "What You'll Do" list at the beginning of each section is your built-in guide to what you need to learn in each chapter. When you can answer the questions in the Section Review and Chapter Review, you know you are ready for a test.

Check Out the Internet

You will see this logo throughout the book. You'll be using *sci*LINKS as your gateway to the Internet. Once you log on to *sci*LINKS using your computer's Internet link, type in the *sci*LINKS address. When asked for the keyword code, type in the keyword for that topic. A wealth of resources is now at your disposal to help you learn more about that topic.

In addition to *sci*LINKS you can log on to some other great resources to go with your text. The addresses shown below will take you to the home page of each site.

---

internet**connect**

This textbook contains the following on-line resources to help you make the most of your science experience.

Visit **go.hrw.com** for extra help and study aids matched to your textbook. Just type in the keyword HST HOME.

Visit **www.scilinks.org** to find resources specific to topics in your textbook. Keywords appear throughout your book to take you further.

Smithsonian Institution®
Internet Connections

Visit **www.si.edu/hrw** for specifically chosen on-line materials from one of our nation's premier science museums.

Visit **www.cnnfyi.com** for late-breaking news and current events stories selected just for you.

Contents   **1**

CHAPTER 1

Chemical Bonding

Sections

Pre-Reading
Questions

1. What is a chemical bond?
2. How are ionic bonds different from covalent bonds?
3. How are the properties of metals related to the type of bonds in them?

BONDED FOR LIFE

Look at the photo. What looks like a fantastic modern art "sculpture" is actually a model of DNA, one of the longest and most complex molecules in living things. In DNA, two very long spiral strands of atoms bond together, forming a double spiral. The DNA in living cells contains all the coding for passing on the traits of that cell and that organism to each new cell as it is formed. In this chapter, you will learn how atoms bond in different ways during chemical reactions.

FROM GLUE TO GOOP

Particles of glue can bond to other particles and hold objects together. Different types of bonds create differences in the properties of substances. In this activity, you will see how the formation of bonds causes an interesting change in the properties of white glue.

Procedure

1. Fill a **small paper cup** $\frac{1}{4}$ full of **white glue.** Observe the properties of the glue, and record your observations.

2. Fill a **second small paper cup** $\frac{1}{4}$ full of **borax solution.**

3. Pour the borax solution into the cup containing the white glue, and stir well using a **plastic spoon.**

4. When it becomes too thick to stir, remove the material from the cup and knead it with your fingers. Observe the properties of the material, and record your observations.

Analysis

5. Compare the properties of the glue with those of the new material.

6. The properties of the new material resulted from the bonds between the borax and the particles of the glue. If too little borax were used, in what way would the properties of the material have been different?

What You'll Do

◆ Describe chemical bonding.
◆ Identify the number of valence electrons in an atom.
◆ Predict whether an atom is likely to form bonds.

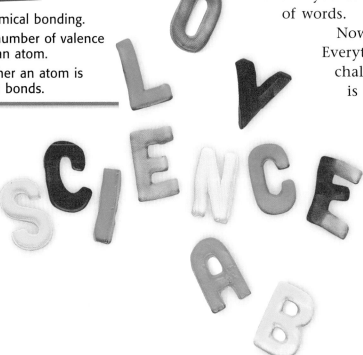

Electrons and Chemical Bonding

Have you ever stopped to consider that by using just the 26 letters of the alphabet, you make all of the words you use every day? Even though the number of letters is limited, their ability to be combined in different ways allows you to make an enormous number of words.

Now look around the room. Everything around you—desks, chalk, paper, even your friends—is made of atoms of elements. How can so many substances be formed from about 100 elements? In the same way that words can be formed by combining letters, different substances can be formed by combining atoms.

Science

C O N N E C T I O N

Why are the amino acids that are chemically bonded together to form your proteins all left-handed? Read about one cosmic explanation on page 24.

Atoms Combine Through Chemical Bonding

The atoms of just three elements—carbon, hydrogen, and oxygen—combine in different patterns to form the substances sugar, alcohol, and citric acid. **Chemical bonding** is the joining of atoms to form new substances. The properties of these new substances are different from those of the original elements. A force of attraction that holds two atoms together is called a **chemical bond.** As you will see, chemical bonds involve the electrons in the atoms.

Atoms and the chemical bonds that connect them cannot be observed with your eyes. During the past 150 years, scientists have performed many experiments that have led to the development of a theory of chemical bonding. Remember that a *theory* is a unifying explanation for a broad range of hypotheses and observations that have been supported by testing. The use of models helps people to discuss the theory of how and why atoms form chemical bonds.

Electron Number and Organization

To understand how atoms form chemical bonds, you first need to know how many electrons are in a particular atom and how the electrons in an atom are organized. The number of electrons in an atom can be determined from the atomic number of the element. The atomic number is the number of protons in an atom. However, atoms have no charge, so the atomic number also represents the number of electrons in the atom.

The electrons in an atom are organized in energy levels. The levels farther from the nucleus contain electrons that have more energy than levels closer to the nucleus. The arrangement of electrons in a chlorine atom is shown in **Figure 1.**

Figure 1 Electron Arrangement in an Atom

ⓐ The **first energy level** is closest to the nucleus and can hold up to 2 electrons.

ⓑ Electrons will enter the **second energy level** only after the first level is full. The second energy level can hold up to 8 electrons.

ⓒ The **third energy level** in this model of a chlorine atom contains only 7 electrons, for a total of 17 electrons in the atom. This outer level of the atom is not full.

Outer-Level Electrons Are the Key to Bonding As you just saw in Figure 1, a chlorine atom has a total of 17 electrons. When a chlorine atom bonds to another atom, not all of these electrons are used to create the bond. Most atoms form bonds using only the electrons in their outermost energy level. The electrons in the outermost energy level of an atom are called **valence** (VAY luhns) **electrons.** Thus, a chlorine atom has 7 valence electrons. You can see the valence electrons for atoms of some other elements in **Figure 2.**

Figure 2 *Valence electrons are the electrons in the outermost energy level of an atom.*

Oxygen
Electron total: 8
First level: 2 electrons
Second level: 6 electrons

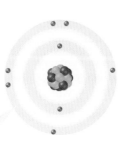

The second energy level is the outermost level, so an oxygen atom has 6 valence electrons.

Sodium
Electron total: 11
First level: 2 electrons
Second level: 8 electrons
Third level: 1 electron

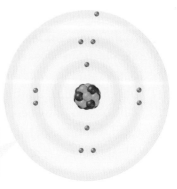

The third energy level is the outermost level, so a sodium atom has 1 valence electron.

Valence Electrons and the Periodic Table You can determine the number of valence electrons in Figure 2 because you have a model to look at. But what if you didn't have a model? You have a tool that helps you determine the number of valence electrons for some elements—the periodic table!

Remember that elements in a group often have similar properties, including the number of electrons in the outermost energy level of their atoms. The number of valence electrons for many elements is related to the group number, as shown in **Figure 3.**

Figure 3 Determining the Number of Valence Electrons

Atoms of elements in **Groups 1 and 2** have the same number of valence electrons as their group number.

Atoms of elements in **Groups 13–18** have 10 fewer valence electrons than their group number. However, helium atoms have only 2 valence electrons.

Atoms of elements in **Groups 3–12** do not have a general rule relating their valence electrons to their group number.

H																	18
1	2											13	14	15	16	17	He
Li	Be											B	C	N	O	F	Ne
Na	Mg	3	4	5	6	7	8	9	10	11	12	Al	Si	P	S	Cl	Ar
K	Ca	Sc	Ti	V	Cr	Mn	Fe	Co	Ni	Cu	Zn	Ga	Ge	As	Se	Br	Kr
Rb	Sr	Y	Zr	Nb	Mo	Tc	Ru	Rh	Pd	Ag	Cd	In	Sn	Sb	Te	I	Xe
Cs	Ba	La	Hf	Ta	W	Re	Os	Ir	Pt	Au	Hg	Tl	Pb	Bi	Po	At	Rn
Fr	Ra	Ac	Rf	Db	Sg	Bh	Hs	Mt	Uun	Uuu	Uub	Uuq		Uuh		Uuo	

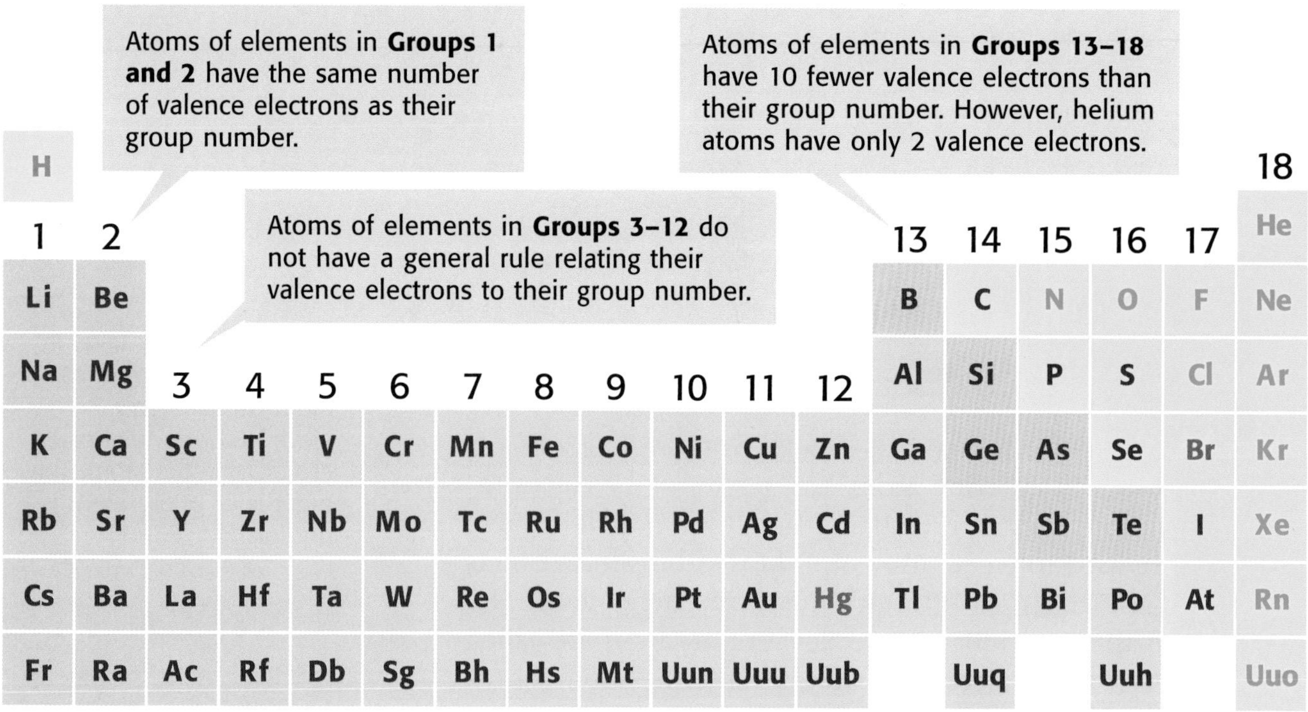

To Bond or Not to Bond

Atoms do not all bond in the same manner. In fact, some atoms rarely bond at all! The number of electrons in the outermost energy level of an atom determines whether an atom will form bonds.

Atoms of the noble, or inert, gases (Group 18) do not normally form chemical bonds. As you just learned, atoms of Group 18 elements (except helium) have 8 valence electrons. Therefore, having 8 valence electrons must be a special condition. In fact, atoms that have 8 electrons in their outermost energy level do not normally form new bonds. The outermost energy level of an atom is considered to be full if it contains 8 electrons.

Activity

Determine the number of valence electrons in each of the following atoms: lithium (Li), beryllium (Be), aluminum (Al), carbon (C), nitrogen (N), sulfur (S), bromine (Br), and krypton (Kr).

TRY at HOME

Atoms Bond to Have a Filled Outermost Level An atom that has fewer than 8 valence electrons is more reactive, or more likely to form bonds, than an atom with 8 valence electrons. Atoms bond by gaining, losing, or sharing electrons in order to have a filled outermost energy level with 8 valence electrons. **Figure 4** describes the ways in which atoms can achieve a filled outermost energy level.

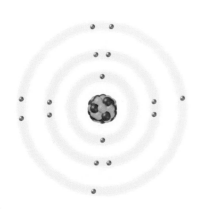

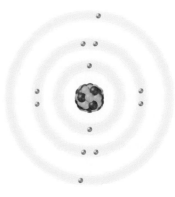

Figure 4 *These atoms achieve a full set of valence electrons in different ways.*

Sulfur

An atom of sulfur has 6 valence electrons. It can have 8 valence electrons by sharing 2 electrons with or gaining 2 electrons from other atoms to fill its outermost energy level.

Magnesium

An atom of magnesium has 2 valence electrons. It can have a full outer level by losing 2 electrons. The second energy level becomes the outermost energy level and contains a full set of 8 electrons.

A Full Set—with Two? Not all atoms need 8 valence electrons for a filled outermost energy level. Helium atoms need only 2 valence electrons. With only 2 electrons in the entire atom, the first energy level (which is also the outermost energy level) is full. Atoms of hydrogen and lithium form bonds with other atoms in order to have 2 electrons.

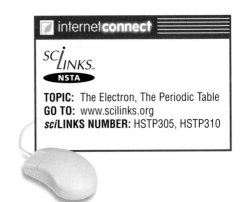

internet connect

*sci*LINKS.
NSTA

TOPIC: The Electron, The Periodic Table
GO TO: www.scilinks.org
*sci*LINKS **NUMBER:** HSTP305, HSTP310

SECTION REVIEW

1. What is a chemical bond?

2. What are valence electrons?

3. How many valence electrons does a silicon atom have?

4. Predict how atoms with 5 valence electrons will achieve a full set of valence electrons.

5. **Interpreting Graphics** At right is a diagram of a fluorine atom. Will fluorine form bonds? Explain.

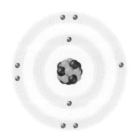

Fluorine

Terms to Learn

ionic bond   covalent bond
ions   molecule
crystal lattice   metallic bond

What You'll Do

◆ Describe ionic, covalent, and
  metallic bonding.
◆ Describe the properties
  associated with substances
  containing each type of bond.

Types of Chemical Bonds

Atoms bond by gaining, losing, or sharing electrons to have a filled outermost energy level containing eight valence electrons. The way in which atoms interact through their valence electrons determines the type of bond that forms. The three types of bonds are ionic (ie AHN ik), covalent (кон VAY luhnt), and metallic.

Ionic Bonds

The materials shown in **Figure 5** have much in common. They are all hard, brittle solids at room temperature, they all have high melting points, and they all contain ionic bonds. An **ionic bond** is the force of attraction between oppositely charged ions. **Ions** are charged particles that form during chemical changes when one or more valence electrons transfer from one atom to another.

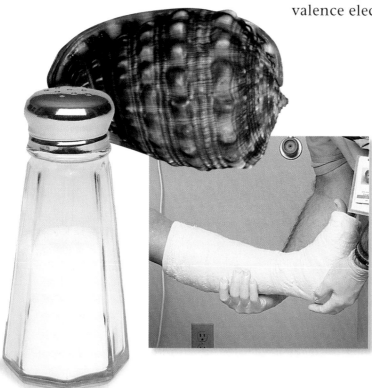

Figure 5 *Calcium carbonate in seashells, sodium chloride in table salt, and calcium sulfate used to make plaster of Paris casts all contain ionic bonds.*

A Transfer of Electrons An atom is neutral because the number of electrons equals the number of protons. So their charges cancel each other. A transfer of electrons between atoms changes the number of electrons in each atom, while the number of protons stays the same. The negative charges and positive charges no longer cancel out, and the atoms become ions. Although an atom cannot gain (or lose) electrons without another atom nearby to lose (or gain) electrons, it is easier to study the formation of ions one at a time.

Atoms That Lose Electrons Form Positive Ions Ionic bonds form during chemical changes when atoms pull electrons away from other atoms. The atoms that lose electrons form ions that have fewer electrons than protons. Because the positive charges outnumber the negative charges, these ions have an overall positive charge.

Metal Atoms Lose Electrons Atoms of most metals have few electrons in their outer energy level. When metal atoms bond with other atoms, the metal atoms tend to lose these valence electrons and form positive ions. For example, look at the model in **Figure 6.** An atom of sodium has one valence electron. When a sodium atom loses this electron to another atom, it becomes a sodium ion. A sodium ion has a charge of 1+ because it contains 1 more proton than electrons. To show the difference between a sodium atom and a sodium ion, the chemical symbol for the ion is written as Na^+. Notice that the charge is written to the upper right of the chemical symbol. Figure 6 also shows a model for the formation of an aluminum ion.

Figure 6   Forming Positive Ions

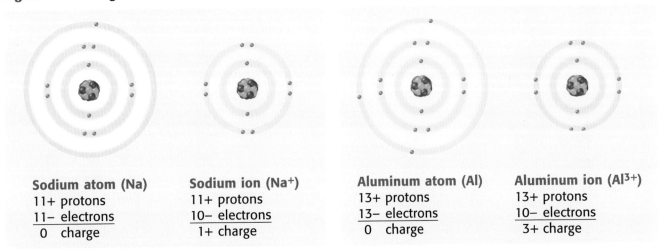

Sodium atom (Na)
11+ protons
11– electrons
―――――――
0   charge

Sodium ion (Na^+)
11+ protons
10– electrons
―――――――
1+ charge

Aluminum atom (Al)
13+ protons
13– electrons
―――――――
0   charge

Aluminum ion (Al^{3+})
13+ protons
10– electrons
―――――――
3+ charge

Here's How It Works: During chemical changes, a sodium atom can lose its 1 electron in the third energy level to another atom. The filled second level becomes the outermost level, so the resulting sodium ion has 8 valence electrons.

Here's How It Works: During chemical changes, an aluminum atom can lose its 3 electrons in the third energy level to another atom. The filled second level becomes the outermost level, so the resulting aluminum ion has 8 valence electrons.

The Energy of Losing Electrons When an atom loses electrons, energy is needed to overcome the attraction between the electrons and the protons in the atom's nucleus. Removing electrons from atoms of metals requires only a small amount of energy, so metal atoms lose electrons easily. In fact, the energy needed to remove electrons from atoms of elements in Groups 1 and 2 is so low that these elements react very easily and can be found only as ions in nature. On the other hand, removing electrons from atoms of nonmetals requires a large amount of energy. Rather than give up electrons, these atoms gain electrons when they form ionic bonds.

Self-Check

Look at the periodic table, and determine which noble gas has the same electron arrangement as a sodium ion. *(See page 136 to check your answer.)*

MATH BREAK

Charge!

Calculating the charge of an ion is the same as adding integers (positive or negative whole numbers or zero) with opposite signs. You write the number of protons as a positive integer and the number of electrons as a negative integer and then add the integers. Calculate the charge of an ion that contains 16 protons and 18 electrons. Write the ion's symbol and name.

Atoms That Gain Electrons Form Negative Ions Atoms that gain electrons from other atoms during chemical changes form ions that have more electrons than protons. The negative charges outnumber the positive charges, giving each of these ions an overall negative charge.

The outermost energy level of nonmetal atoms is almost full. Only a few electrons are needed to fill the outer level, so atoms of nonmetals tend to gain electrons from other atoms. For example, look at the model in **Figure 7.** An atom of chlorine has 7 valence electrons. When a chlorine atom gains 1 electron to complete its outer level, it becomes an ion with a 1– charge called a chloride ion. The symbol for the chloride ion is Cl^-. Notice that the name of the negative ion formed from chlorine has the ending *-ide*. This ending is used for the names of the negative ions formed when atoms gain electrons. Figure 7 also shows a model of how an oxide ion is formed.

Figure 7 Forming Negative Ions

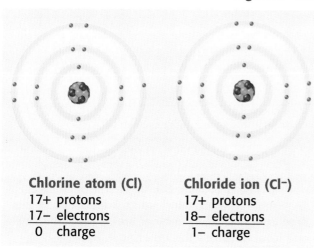

Chlorine atom (Cl)
17+ protons
17– electrons
0 charge

Chloride ion (Cl⁻)
17+ protons
18– electrons
1– charge

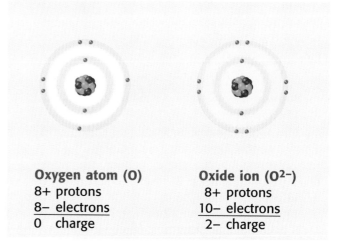

Oxygen atom (O)
8+ protons
8– electrons
0 charge

Oxide ion (O²⁻)
8+ protons
10– electrons
2– charge

Here's How It Works: During chemical changes, a chlorine atom gains 1 electron in the third energy level from another atom. A chloride ion is formed with 8 valence electrons. Thus, its outermost energy level is filled.

Here's How It Works: During chemical changes, an oxygen atom gains 2 electrons in the second energy level from another atom. An oxide ion is formed with 8 valence electrons. Thus, its outermost energy level is filled.

The Energy of Gaining Electrons Atoms of most nonmetals fill their outermost energy level by gaining electrons. Energy is given off by most nonmetal atoms during this process. The more easily an atom gains an electron, the more energy an atom gives off. Atoms of the Group 17 elements (the halogens) give off the most energy when they gain an electron. The halogens, such as fluorine and chlorine, are extremely reactive nonmetals because they release a large amount of energy.

Charged Ions Form a Neutral Compound When a metal reacts with a nonmetal, the same number of electrons is lost by the metal atoms as is gained by the nonmetal atoms. Even though the ions that bond are charged, the compound formed is neutral because the charges of the ions cancel each other through ionic bonding. An ionic bond is an example of electrostatic attraction in which opposite electric charges stick together. Another example is static cling, illustrated in **Figure 8.**

Figure 8 *Like ionic bonds, static cling is the result of the attraction between opposite charges.*

Ions Bond to Form a Crystal Lattice The ions that make up an ionic compound are bonded in a repeating three-dimensional pattern called a **crystal lattice** (KRI stuhl LAT is). In ionic compounds, such as table salt, the ions in the crystal lattice are arranged as alternating positive and negative ions, forming a solid. The model in **Figure 9** shows a small part of a crystal lattice. The arrangement of bonded ions in a crystal lattice determines the shape of the crystals of an ionic compound.

The strong force of attraction between bonded ions in a crystal lattice gives ionic compounds certain properties, including a high melting point and boiling point. Ionic compounds tend to be brittle solids at room temperature and usually break apart when hit with a hammer.

Figure 9 *This model of the crystal lattice of sodium chloride, or table salt, shows a three-dimensional view of the bonded ions.*

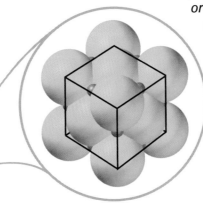

SECTION REVIEW

1. How does an atom become a negative ion?

2. What are two properties of ionic compounds?

3. **Applying Concepts** Which group of elements lose 2 valence electrons when their atoms form ionic bonds? What charge would the ions formed have?

Covalent Bonds

Most materials you encounter every day, such as water, sugar, and carbon dioxide, are held together by bonds that do not involve ions. These substances tend to have low melting and boiling points, and some of these substances are brittle in the solid state. The type of bonds found in these substances, including the substances shown in **Figure 10,** are covalent bonds.

A **covalent bond** is the force of attraction between the nuclei of atoms and the electrons shared by the atoms. When two atoms of nonmetals bond, a large amount of energy is required for either atom to lose an electron, so no ions are formed. Rather than transferring electrons to complete their outermost energy levels, two nonmetal atoms bond by sharing electrons with one another, as shown in the model in **Figure 11.**

Figure 10 *Covalent bonds are found in this plastic ball, the paddle's rubber covering, the cotton fibers in clothes, and even many of the substances that make up the human body!*

Figure 11 *By sharing electrons in a covalent bond, each hydrogen atom (the smallest atom known) has a full outermost energy level containing two electrons.*

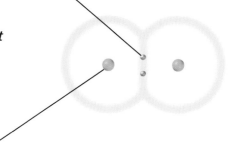

The shared electrons spend most of their time between the nuclei of the atoms.

The protons and the shared electrons attract one another. This attraction is the basis of the covalent bond that holds the atoms together.

Covalently Bonded Atoms Make Up Molecules The particles of substances containing covalent bonds differ from those containing ionic bonds. Ionic compounds consist of ions organized in a crystal. Covalent compounds consist of individual particles called molecules (MAHL i KYOOLZ). A **molecule** is a neutral group of atoms held together by covalent bonds. In Figure 11, you saw a model of a hydrogen molecule, which is composed of two hydrogen atoms covalently bonded. However, most molecules are composed of atoms of two or more elements. The models in **Figure 12** show two ways to represent the covalent bonds in a molecule.

Figure 12 Covalent Bonds in a Water Molecule

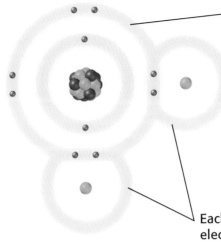

Through covalent bonding, the oxygen atom shares one of its electrons with each of the two hydrogen atoms. As a result, it has a filled outermost energy level with 8 electrons.

Each hydrogen atom shares its 1 electron with the oxygen atom. This allows each hydrogen to have a filled outer level with 2 electrons.

Another way to show covalent bonds is to draw an electron-dot diagram. An electron-dot diagram shows only the outermost level of electrons for each atom. But you can still see how electrons are shared between the atoms.

Making Electron-Dot Diagrams

An electron-dot diagram is a model that shows only the valence electrons in an atom. Electron-dot diagrams are helpful when predicting how atoms might bond. You draw an electron-dot diagram by writing the symbol of the element and placing the correct number of dots around it. This type of model can help you to better understand bonding by showing the number of valence electrons and how atoms share electrons to fill their outermost energy levels, as shown below.

Carbon atoms have 4 valence electrons, so 4 dots are placed around the symbol. A carbon atom needs 4 more electrons for a filled outermost energy level.

Oxygen atoms have 6 valence electrons, so 6 dots are placed around the symbol. An oxygen atom needs only 2 more electrons for a filled outermost energy level.

The noble gas krypton has a full set of 8 valence electrons in its atoms. Thus, krypton is nonreactive because its atoms do not need any more electrons.

This electron-dot diagram represents hydrogen gas, the same substance shown in the model in Figure 11.

Self-Check

1. How many dots does the electron-dot diagram of a sulfur atom have?
2. How is a covalent bond different from an ionic bond?
   (See page 136 to check your answers.)

Figure 13 *The water in this fishbowl is made up of many tiny water molecules. Each molecule is the smallest particle that still has the chemical properties of water.*

A Molecule Is the Smallest Particle of a Covalent Compound An atom is the smallest particle into which an element can be divided and still be the same substance. Likewise, a molecule is the smallest particle into which a covalently bonded compound can be divided and still be the same compound. **Figure 13** illustrates how a sample of water is made up of many individual molecules of water (shown as three-dimensional models). If you could divide water over and over, you would eventually end up with a single molecule of water. However, if you separated the hydrogen and oxygen atoms that make up a water molecule, you would no longer have water.

The Simplest Molecules All molecules are composed of at least two covalently bonded atoms. The simplest molecules, known as *diatomic molecules,* consist of two atoms bonded together. Some elements are called diatomic elements because they are found in nature as diatomic molecules composed of two atoms of the element. Hydrogen is a diatomic element, as you saw in Figure 11. Oxygen, nitrogen, and the halogens fluorine, chlorine, bromine, and iodine are also diatomic. By sharing electrons, both atoms of a diatomic molecule can fill their outer energy level, as shown in **Figure 14.**

Activity

Try your hand at drawing electron-dot diagrams for a molecule of chlorine (a diatomic molecule) and a molecule of ammonia (one nitrogen atom bonded with three hydrogen atoms).

TRY at HOME

Figure 14 Models of a Diatomic Fluorine Molecule

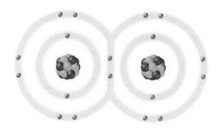

Two covalently bonded fluorine atoms have filled outermost energy levels. The pair of electrons shared by the atoms are counted as valence electrons for each atom.

This is a three-dimensional model of a fluorine molecule.

More-Complex Molecules Diatomic molecules are the simplest—and some of the most important—of all molecules. You could not live without diatomic oxygen molecules. But other important molecules are much more complex. Gasoline, plastic, and even proteins in the cells of your body are examples of complex molecules. Carbon atoms are the basis of many of these complex molecules. Each carbon atom needs to make 4 covalent bonds to have 8 valence electrons. These bonds can be with atoms of other elements or with other carbon atoms, as shown in the model in **Figure 15.**

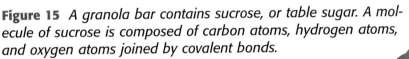
Biology
C O N N E C T I O N

Proteins perform many functions throughout your body, such as digesting your food, building components of your cells, and transporting nutrients to each cell. A single protein can have a chain of 7,000 atoms of carbon and nitrogen with atoms of other elements covalently bonded to it.

Figure 15 *A granola bar contains sucrose, or table sugar. A molecule of sucrose is composed of carbon atoms, hydrogen atoms, and oxygen atoms joined by covalent bonds.*

Hydrogen

Carbon

Oxygen

Metallic Bonds

Look at the unusual metal sculpture shown in **Figure 16.** Notice that some metal pieces have been flattened, while other metal pieces have been shaped into wires. How could the artist change the shape of the metal into all of these different forms without breaking the metal into pieces? A metal can be shaped because of the presence of a special type of bond called a metallic bond. A **metallic bond** is the force of attraction between a positively charged metal ion and the electrons in a metal. (Remember that metal atoms tend to lose electrons and form positively charged ions.)

Figure 16 *The different shapes of metal in this sculpture are possible because of the bonds that hold the metal together.*

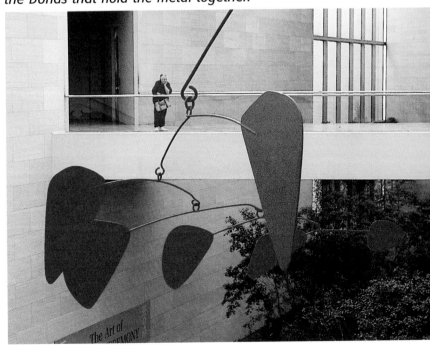

Bending with Bonds

1. Straighten out a **wire paper clip.** Record the result in your ScienceLog.

2. Bend a **piece of chalk.** Record the result in your ScienceLog.

3. Chalk is composed of calcium carbonate, a compound containing ionic bonds. What type of bonds are present in the paper clip?

4. In your ScienceLog, explain why you could change the shape of the paper clip but could not bend the chalk without breaking it.

BRAIN FOOD

Gold can be pounded out to make a foil only a few atoms thick. A piece of gold the size of the head of a pin can be beaten into a thin "leaf" that would cover this page!

Electrons Move Throughout a Metal The scientific understanding of the bonding in metals is that the metal atoms get so close to one another that their outermost energy levels overlap. This allows their valence electrons to move throughout the metal from the energy level of one atom to the energy levels of the atoms nearby. The atoms form a crystal much like the ions associated with ionic bonding. However, the negative charges (electrons) in the metal are free to move about. You can think of a metal as being made up of positive metal ions with enough valence electrons "swimming" about to keep the ions together and to cancel the positive charge of the ions, as shown in **Figure 17.** The ions are held together because metallic bonds extend throughout the metal in all directions.

Figure 17 *The moving electrons are attracted to the metal ions, forming metallic bonds.*

The positive metal ions are in fixed positions in the metal.

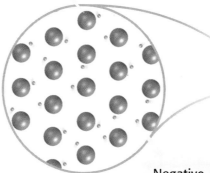

Negative electrons are free to move about.

Metals Conduct Electric Current Metallic bonding is the reason why metals have particular properties. One of these properties is electrical conductivity—the ability to conduct electric current. For example, when you turn on a lamp, electrons move within the copper wire that connects the lamp with the outlet. The electrons that move are the valence electrons in the copper atoms. These electrons are free to move because of metallic bonds—they are not connected to any one atom.

Metals Can Be Reshaped Metallic bonds allow atoms in metals to be rearranged. As a result, metals can be reshaped. The properties of *ductility* (the ability to be drawn into wires) and *malleability* (the ability to be hammered into sheets) describe a metal's ability to be reshaped. For example, copper is made into wires for use in electrical cords. Aluminum can be pounded into thin sheets and made into aluminum foil and cans.

How Metals Can Bend Without Breaking When a piece of metal is bent, some of the metal ions are forced closer together. You might expect the metal to break because the positive ions repel one another. However, even in their new positions, the positive ions are surrounded by and attracted to the electrons, as shown in **Figure 18.** (Ionic compounds do break when hit because neither the positive ions nor the negative ions are free to move.)

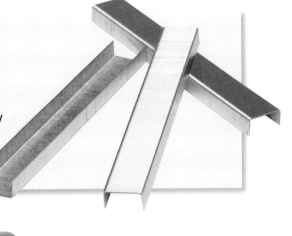

Figure 18 *The shape of a metal can be changed without breaking because metallic bonds occur in many directions.*

The repulsion between the positively charged metal ions increases as the ions are pushed closer to one another.

The moving electrons maintain the metallic bonds no matter how the shape of the metal changes.

Metallic Bonding in Staples

Although they are not very glamorous, metal staples are very useful in holding things such as sheets of paper together. Explain how the metallic bonds in a staple allow it to change shape so that it can function properly.

SECTION REVIEW

1. What happens to electrons in covalent bonding?

2. What type of element is most likely to form covalent bonds?

3. What is a metallic bond?

4. **Interpreting Graphics** This electron-dot diagram is not yet complete. Which atom needs to form another covalent bond? How do you know?

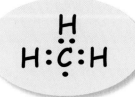

■ internet**connect**

SC*L*INKS.
NSTA

TOPIC: Types of Chemical Bonds, Properties of Metals
GO TO: www.scilinks.org
*sci*LINKS NUMBER: HSTP315, HSTP320

Making Models Lab

Covalent Marshmallows

A hydrogen atom has one electron in its outer energy level, but two electrons are required to fill its outer level. An oxygen atom has six electrons in its outer energy level, but eight electrons are required to fill its outer level. In order to fill their outer energy levels, two atoms of hydrogen and one atom of oxygen can share electrons, as shown below. Such a sharing of electrons to fill the outer level of atoms is called **covalent bonding**. When hydrogen and oxygen bond in this manner, a molecule of water is formed. In this lab, you will build a three-dimensional model of water in order to better understand the covalent bonds formed in a water molecule.

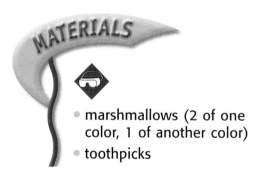

- marshmallows (2 of one color, 1 of another color)
- toothpicks

Procedure

1 Using the marshmallows and toothpicks, create a model of a water molecule. Use the diagram below for guidance in building your model.

2 Sketch your model in your ScienceLog. Be sure to label the hydrogen and oxygen atoms on your sketch.

3 Draw an electron-dot diagram of the water molecule in your ScienceLog. (Refer to the chapter text if you need help drawing an electron-dot diagram.)

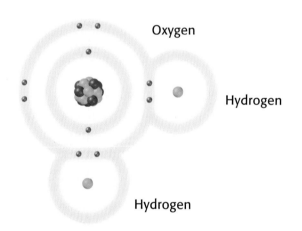

A Model of a Water Molecule

Analysis

4 What do the marshmallows represent? What do the toothpicks represent?

5 Why are the marshmallows different colors?

6 Compare your model with the picture above. How might your model be improved to more accurately represent a water molecule?

7 Hydrogen in nature can covalently bond to form hydrogen molecules, H_2. How could you model this using the marshmallows and toothpicks?

8 Draw an electron-dot diagram of a hydrogen molecule in your ScienceLog.

9 Which do you think would be more difficult to create—a model of an ionic bond or a model of a covalent bond? Explain your answer.

Going Further

Create a model of a carbon dioxide molecule, which consists of two oxygen atoms and one carbon atom. The structure is similar to the structure of water, although the three atoms bond in a straight line instead of at angles. The bond between each oxygen atom and the carbon atom in a carbon dioxide molecule is a "double bond," so use two connections. Do the double bonds in carbon dioxide appear stronger or weaker than the single bonds in water? Explain your answer.

Chapter Highlights

Vocabulary

chemical bonding *(p. 4)*

chemical bond *(p. 4)*

valence electrons *(p. 5)*

Section Notes

• Chemical bonding is the joining of atoms to form new substances. A chemical bond is a force of attraction that holds two atoms together.

• Valence electrons are the electrons in the outermost energy level of an atom. These electrons are used to form bonds.

• Most atoms form bonds by gaining, losing, or sharing electrons until they have 8 valence electrons. Atoms of hydrogen, lithium, and helium need only 2 electrons to fill their outermost level.

Vocabulary

ionic bond *(p. 8)*

ions *(p. 8)*

crystal lattice *(p. 11)*

covalent bond *(p. 12)*

molecule *(p. 12)*

metallic bond *(p. 15)*

Section Notes

• In ionic bonding, electrons are transferred between two atoms. The atom that loses electrons becomes a positive ion. The atom that gains electrons becomes a negative ion. The force of attraction between these oppositely charged ions is an ionic bond.

• Ionic bonding usually occurs between atoms of metals and atoms of nonmetals.

☑ Skills Check

Math Concepts

CALCULATING CHARGE To calculate the charge of an ion, you must add integers with opposite signs. The total positive charge of the ion (the number of protons) is written as a positive integer. The total negative charge of the ion (the number of electrons) is written as a negative integer. For example, the charge of an ion containing 11 protons and 10 electrons would be calculated as follows:

$$(11+) + (10-) = 1+$$

Visual Understanding

DETERMINING VALENCE ELECTRONS Knowing the number of valence electrons in an atom is important in predicting how it will bond with other atoms. Review Figure 3 on page 6 to learn how an element's location on the periodic table helps you determine the number of valence electrons in an atom.

FORMING IONS Turn back to Figures 6 and 7 on pages 9–10 to review how ions are formed when atoms lose or gain electrons.

- Energy is needed to remove electrons from metal atoms to form positive ions. Energy is released when most nonmetal atoms gain electrons to form negative ions.

- In covalent bonding, electrons are shared by two atoms. The force of attraction between the nuclei of the atoms and the shared electrons is a covalent bond.

- Covalent bonding usually occurs between atoms of nonmetals.

- Electron-dot diagrams are a simple way to represent the valence electrons in an atom.

- Covalently bonded atoms form a particle called a molecule. A molecule is the smallest particle of a compound with the chemical properties of the compound.

- Diatomic elements are the only elements found in nature as diatomic molecules consisting of two atoms of the same element covalently bonded together.

- In metallic bonding, the outermost energy levels of metal atoms overlap, allowing the valence electrons to move throughout the metal. The force of attraction between a positive metal ion and the electrons in the metal is a metallic bond.

- Many properties of metals, such as conductivity, ductility, and malleability, result from the freely moving electrons in the metal.

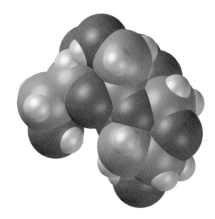

 internetconnect

GO TO: go.hrw.com

Visit the **HRW** Web site for a variety of learning tools related to this chapter. Just type in the keyword:

KEYWORD: HSTBND

 SCILINKS℠ NSTA

GO TO: www.scilinks.org

Visit the **National Science Teachers Association** on-line Web site for Internet resources related to this chapter. Just type in the sciLINKS number for more information about the topic:

TOPIC: The Electron	sciLINKS NUMBER: HSTP305
TOPIC: The Periodic Table	sciLINKS NUMBER: HSTP310
TOPIC: Types of Chemical Bonds	sciLINKS NUMBER: HSTP315
TOPIC: Properties of Metals	sciLINKS NUMBER: HSTP320

Chapter Review

USING VOCABULARY

To complete the following sentences, choose the correct term from each pair of terms listed below.

1. The force of attraction that holds two atoms together is a ____. *(crystal lattice* or *chemical bond)*

2. Charged particles that form when atoms transfer electrons are ____. *(molecules* or *ions)*

3. The force of attraction between the nuclei of atoms and shared electrons is a(n) ____. *(ionic bond* or *covalent bond)*

4. Electrons free to move throughout a material are associated with a(n) ____. *(ionic bond* or *metallic bond)*

5. Shared electrons are associated with a ____. *(covalent bond* or *metallic bond)*

UNDERSTANDING CONCEPTS

Multiple Choice

6. Which element has a full outermost energy level containing only two electrons?
   a. oxygen (O)   c. fluorine (F)
   b. hydrogen (H)   d. helium (He)

7. Which of the following describes what happens when an atom becomes an ion with a 2– charge?
   a. The atom gains 2 protons.
   b. The atom loses 2 protons.
   c. The atom gains 2 electrons.
   d. The atom loses 2 electrons.

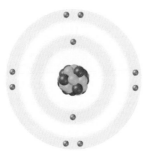

8. The properties of ductility and malleability are associated with which type of bonds?
   a. ionic
   b. covalent
   c. metallic
   d. none of the above

9. In which area of the periodic table do you find elements whose atoms easily gain electrons?
   a. across the top two rows
   b. across the bottom row
   c. on the right side
   d. on the left side

10. What type of element tends to lose electrons when it forms bonds?
    a. metal
    b. metalloid
    c. nonmetal
    d. noble gas

11. Which pair of atoms can form an ionic bond?
    a. sodium (Na) and potassium (K)
    b. potassium (K) and fluorine (F)
    c. fluorine (F) and chlorine (Cl)
    d. sodium (Na) and neon (Ne)

Short Answer

12. List two properties of covalent compounds.

13. Explain why an iron ion is attracted to a sulfide ion but not to a zinc ion.

14. Using your knowledge of valence electrons, explain the main reason so many different molecules are made from carbon atoms.

15. Compare the three types of bonds based on what happens to the valence electrons of the atoms.

Concept Mapping

16. Use the following terms to create a concept map: chemical bonds, ionic bonds, covalent bonds, metallic bonds, molecule, ions.

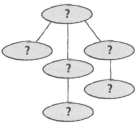

20. For each atom below, write the number of electrons it must gain or lose to have 8 valence electrons. Then calculate the charge of the ion that would form.
    a. calcium (Ca)
    b. phosphorus (P)
    c. bromine (Br)
    d. sulfur (S)

CRITICAL THINKING AND PROBLEM SOLVING

17. Predict the type of bond each of the following pairs of atoms would form:
    a. zinc (Zn) and zinc (Zn)
    b. oxygen (O) and nitrogen (N)
    c. phosphorus (P) and oxygen (O)
    d. magnesium (Mg) and chlorine (Cl)

18. Draw electron-dot diagrams for each of the following atoms, and state how many bonds it will have to make to fill its outer energy level.
    a. sulfur (S)
    b. nitrogen (N)
    c. neon (Ne)
    d. iodine (I)
    e. silicon (Si)

19. Does the substance being hit in the photo below contain ionic or metallic bonds? Explain.

INTERPRETING GRAPHICS

Look at the picture of the wooden pencil below, and answer the following questions.

21. In which part of the pencil are metallic bonds found?

22. List three materials composed of molecules with covalent bonds.

23. Identify two differences between the properties of the metallically bonded material and one of the covalently bonded materials.

Reading Check-up

Take a minute to review your answers to the Pre-Reading Questions found at the bottom of page 2. Have your answers changed? If necessary, revise your answers based on what you have learned since you began this chapter.

Left-Handed Molecules

Some researchers think that light from a newly forming star 1,500 light-years away (1 light-year is equal to about 9.6 trillion kilometers) may hold the answer to an Earthly riddle that has been puzzling scientists for over 100 years!

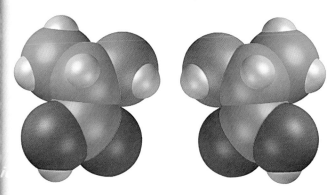

▲ *Molecules, such as the carbon molecules shown above, often come in two mirror-image forms, just as hands do.*

We Are All Lefties!

In 1848, Louis Pasteur discovered that carbon-containing molecules come in left-handed and right-handed forms. Each of the molecules is an exact mirror image of the other, just as each of your hands is a mirror image of the other. These molecules are made of the same elements, but they differ in the elements' arrangement in space.

Shortly after Pasteur's discovery, researchers stumbled across an interesting but unexplained phenomenon—all organisms, including humans, are made almost entirely of left-handed molecules! Chemists were puzzled by this observation because when they made amino acids in the laboratory, the amino acids came out in equal numbers of right- and left-handed forms. Scientists also found that organisms cannot even use the right-handed form of the amino acids to make proteins! For years, scientists have tried to explain this. Why are biological molecules usually left-handed and not right-handed?

Cosmic Explanation

Astronomers recently discovered that a newly forming star in the constellation Orion emits a unique type of infrared light. Infrared light has a wavelength longer than the wavelength of visible light. The wave particles of this light spiral through space like a corkscrew. This light spirals in only one direction. Researchers suspect that this light might give clues to why all organisms are lefties.

Laboratory experiments show that depending on the direction of the ultraviolet light spirals, either left-handed or right-handed molecules are destroyed. Scientists wonder if a similar type of light may have been present when life was beginning on Earth. Such light may have destroyed most right-handed molecules, which explains why life's molecules are left-handed.

Skeptics argue that the infrared light has less energy than the ultraviolet light used in the laboratory experiments and thus is not a valid comparison. Some researchers, however, hypothesize that both infrared and ultraviolet light may be emitted from the newly forming star that is 1,500 light-years away.

Find Out More

▶ The French chemist Pasteur discovered left-handed and right-handed molecules in tartaric acid. Do some research to find out more about Pasteur and his discovery. Share your findings with the class.

Eureka!

Here's Looking At Ya'!

To some people, just the thought of putting small pieces of plastic in their eyes is uncomfortable. But for millions of others, those little pieces of plastic, known as contact lenses, are a part of daily life. So what would you think about putting a piece of glass in your eye instead? Strangely enough, the humble beginning of the contact lens began with doing just that—inserting a glass lens right in the eye! Ouch!

Molded Glass

Early developers of contact lenses had only glass to use until plastics were discovered. In 1929, a Hungarian physician named Joseph Dallos came up with a way to make a mold of the human eye. This was a critical step in the development of contact lenses. He used these molds to make a glass lens that followed the shape of the eye rather than laying flat against it. In combination with the eye's natural lens, light was refocused to improve a person's eyesight. As you can probably guess, glass lenses weren't very comfortable.

Still Too Hard

Seven years later, an American optometrist, William Feinbloom, introduced contact lenses made of hard plastic. Plastic was a newly developed material made from long, stable chains of carbon, hydrogen, and oxygen molecules called polymers. But polymers required a lot of work to make. Chemists heated short chains, forcing them to chemically bond to form a longer, more-stable polymer. The whole process was also expensive. To make matters worse, the hard-plastic lenses made from polymers weren't much more comfortable than the glass lenses.

How About Spinning Plastic Gel?

In an effort to solve the comfort problem, Czech chemists Otto Wichterle and Drahoslav Lim invented a water-absorbing plastic gel. The lenses made from this gel were soft and pliable, and they allowed air to pass through the lens to the eye. These characteristics made the lenses much more comfortable to wear than the glass lenses.

Wichterle solved the cost problem by developing a simple and inexpensive process to make the plastic-gel lenses. In this process, called spin casting, liquid plastic is added to a spinning mold of an eye. When the plastic forms the correct shape, it is treated with ultraviolet and infrared light, which hardens the plastic. Both plastic gel and spin casting were patented in 1963, becoming the foundation for the contact lenses people wear today.

Look Toward the Future

▶ What do you think contact lenses might be like in 20 years? Let your imagination run wild. Sometimes the strangest ideas are the best seeds of new inventions!

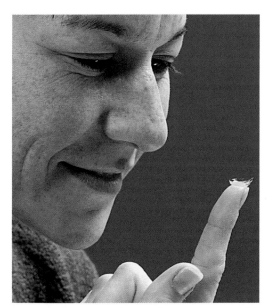
▲ *Does the thought of putting something in your eye make you squirm?*

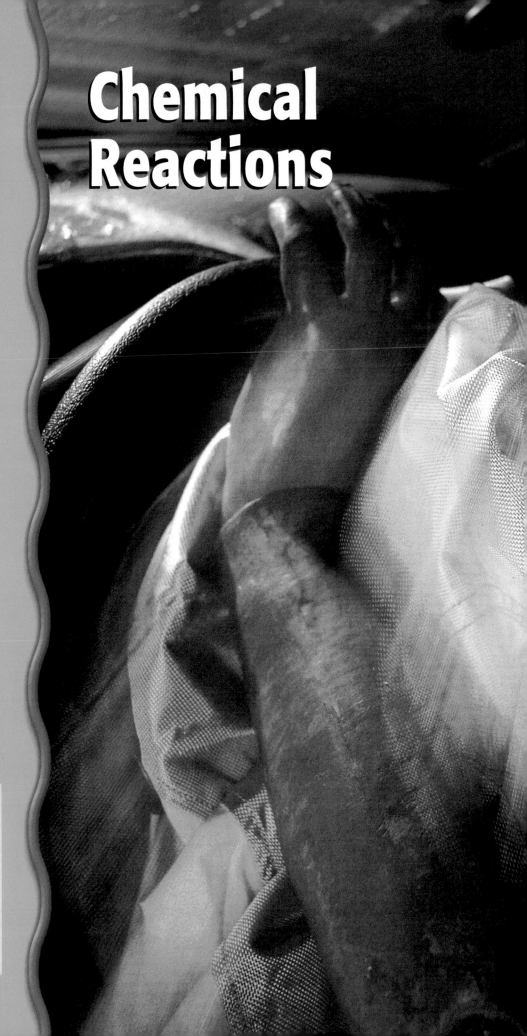

CHAPTER 2

Chemical Reactions

Pre-Reading
Questions

1. What clues can help
   you identify a chemical
   reaction?

2. What are some types of
   chemical reactions?

3. How can you change the
   rate of a chemical reaction?

REACTION TO THE RESCUE

A car slams into a wall at 97 km/h (60 mi/h) during a crash test. Although both dummies are wearing seat belts, one suffers a crushing blow to the head as it strikes the dashboard. The other suffers only minor bruises, thanks to an air bag. Air bags can inflate rapidly because of a chemical reaction that produces gas at a very fast rate. In this chapter, you will learn how to identify and describe a chemical reaction. You will also learn about factors that affect the rate of a reaction.

START-UP Activity

A MODEL FORMULA

Chemicals react in very precise ways. In this activity, you will model a chemical reaction and predict how chemicals react.

Procedure

1. You will receive **several models** that are made from marshmallows stuck together with toothpicks. Each of these models is a Model A.

2. Your teacher will show you Model B and Model C. Take apart one or more Model A's to make copies of model B and Model C.

3. Do you have any pieces left over? If so, use them to make more Model B's and/or Model C's. Do you need more parts to complete Model B or Model C? If so, take apart another Model A.

4. If necessary, repeat step 3 until you have no parts left over.

Analysis

5. How many Model A's did you use to make copies of Model B and Model C?

6. How many Model B's did you make? How many Model C's did you make?

7. Suppose you needed to make six Model B's. How many Model A's would you need? How many Model C's could you make with the leftover parts?

Forming New Substances

Terms to Learn

chemical reaction
chemical formula
chemical equation
reactants
products
law of conservation of mass

What You'll Do

◆ Identify the clues that indicate a chemical reaction might be taking place.
◆ Interpret and write simple chemical formulas.
◆ Interpret and write simple balanced chemical equations.
◆ Explain how a balanced equation illustrates the law of conservation of mass.

Each fall, an amazing transformation takes place. Leaves change color, as shown in **Figure 1.** Vibrant reds, oranges, and yellows that had been hidden by green all year are seen as the temperatures get cooler and the hours of sunlight become fewer. What is happening to cause this change? Leaves have a green color as a result of a compound called chlorophyll (KLOR uh FIL). Each fall, the chlorophyll undergoes a chemical change and forms simpler substances that have no color. You can see the red, orange, and yellow colors in the leaves because the green color of the chlorophyll no longer hides them.

Figure 1 *The change of color in the fall is a result of chemical changes in the leaves.*

Chemical Reactions

The chemical change that occurs as chlorophyll breaks down into simpler substances is one example of a chemical reaction. A **chemical reaction** is the process by which one or more substances undergo change to produce one or more different substances. These new substances have different chemical and physical properties from the original substances. Many of the changes you are familiar with are chemical reactions, including the ones shown in **Figure 2.**

Figure 2 Examples of Chemical Reactions

The substances that make up baking powder undergo a chemical reaction when mixed with water. One new substance that forms is carbon dioxide gas, which causes the bubbles in this muffin.

Once ignited, gasoline reacts with oxygen gas in the air. The new substances that form, carbon dioxide and water, push against the pistons in the engine to keep the car moving.

Clues to Chemical Reactions How can you tell when a chemical reaction is taking place? There are several clues that indicate when a reaction might be occurring. The more of these clues you observe, the more likely it is that the change is a chemical reaction. Several of these clues are described below.

Some Clues to Chemical Reactions

Gas Formation
The formation of gas bubbles is a clue that a chemical reaction might be taking place. For example, bubbles of carbon dioxide are produced when hydrochloric acid is placed on a piece of limestone.

Solid Formation
A solid formed in a solution as a result of a chemical reaction is called a *precipitate* (pruh SIP uh TAYT). Here you see potassium chromate solution being added to a silver nitrate solution. The dark red solid is a precipitate of silver chromate.

Color Change
Chlorine bleach is great for removing the color from stains on white clothes. But don't spill it on your jeans. The bleach reacts with the blue dye on the fabric, causing the color of the material to change.

Energy Change
Energy is released during some chemical reactions. A fire heats a room and provides light. Electrical energy is released when chemicals in a battery react. During some other chemical reactions, energy is absorbed. Chemicals on photographic film react when they absorb energy from light shining on the film.

Breaking and Making Bonds New substances are formed in a chemical reaction because chemical bonds in the starting substances break, atoms rearrange, and new bonds form to make the new substances. Look at the model in **Figure 3** to understand how this process occurs.

Figure 3
Reaction of Hydrogen and Chlorine

Breaking Bonds The elements hydrogen and chlorine are diatomic, meaning they are composed of molecules that consist of two atoms bonded together. For these molecules to react, the bonds joining the atoms must break.

Making Bonds Molecules of the new substance, hydrogen chloride, are formed as new bonds are made between hydrogen atoms and chlorine atoms.

Chemical Formulas

Remember that a chemical symbol is a shorthand method of identifying an element. A **chemical formula** is a shorthand notation for a compound or a diatomic element using chemical symbols and numbers. A chemical formula indicates the chemical makeup by showing how many of each kind of atom is present in a molecule.

The chemical formula for water, H_2O, tells you that a water molecule is composed of two atoms of hydrogen and one atom of oxygen. The small number *2* in the formula is a subscript. A *subscript* is a number written below and to the right of a chemical symbol in a formula. When no subscript is written after a symbol, as with the oxygen in water's formula, only one atom of that element is present. **Figure 4** shows two more chemical formulas and what they mean.

$\div$ 5 $\div$ Ω $\leq$ ∞ $+\Omega$ $\sqrt{}$ 9 ∞ $\leq$ Σ 2

MATH BREAK

Counting Atoms

Some chemical formulas contain two or more chemical symbols enclosed by parentheses. When counting atoms in these formulas, multiply everything inside the parentheses by the subscript as though they were part of a mathematical equation. For example, $Ca(NO_3)_2$ contains:

1 calcium atom
2 nitrogen atoms (2 × 1)
6 oxygen atoms (2 × 3)

Now It's Your Turn

Determine the number of atoms of each element in the formulas $Mg(OH)_2$ and $Al_2(SO_4)_3$.

Figure 4 *A chemical formula shows the number of atoms of each element present.*

$$O_2$$

$$C_6H_{12}O_6$$

Oxygen is a diatomic element. Each molecule of oxygen gas is composed of two atoms of oxygen bonded together.

Every molecule of **glucose** (the sugar formed by plants during photosynthesis) is composed of six atoms of carbon, twelve atoms of hydrogen, and six atoms of oxygen.

Writing Formulas for Covalent Compounds You can often write a chemical formula if you know the name of the substance. Remember that covalent compounds are usually composed of two nonmetals. The names of covalent compounds use prefixes to tell you how many atoms of each element are in the formula. A *prefix* is a syllable or syllables joined to the beginning of a word. Each prefix used in a chemical name represents a number, as shown in the table at right. **Figure 5** demonstrates how to write a chemical formula from the name of a covalent compound.

Prefixes Used in Chemical Names			
mono-	1	hexa-	6
di-	2	hepta-	7
tri-	3	octa-	8
tetra-	4	nona-	9
penta-	5	deca-	10

Carbon dioxide

$$CO_2$$

The *lack of a prefix* indicates 1 carbon atom.

The prefix *di-* indicates 2 oxygen atoms.

Dinitrogen monoxide

$$N_2O$$

The prefix *di-* indicates 2 nitrogen atoms.

The prefix *mono-* indicates 1 oxygen atom.

Figure 5 *The formulas of these covalent compounds can be written using the prefixes in their names.*

Self-Check

How many atoms of each element make up Na_2SO_4?
(See page 136 to check your answer.)

Writing Formulas for Ionic Compounds If the name of a compound contains the name of a metal and a nonmetal, the compound is probably ionic. To write the formula for an ionic compound, you must make sure the compound's overall charge is zero. In other words, the formula must have subscripts that cause the charges of the ions to cancel out. (Remember that the charge of many ions can be determined by looking at the periodic table.) **Figure 6** demonstrates how to write a chemical formula from the name of an ionic compound.

Figure 6 *The formula of an ionic compound is written by using enough of each ion so the overall charge is zero.*

Sodium chloride

$$NaCl$$

A sodium ion has a 1+ **charge.**
A chloride ion has a 1− **charge.**

One sodium ion and one chloride ion have an overall **charge of (1+) + (1−) = 0**

Magnesium chloride

$$MgCl_2$$

A magnesium ion has a 2+ **charge.**
A chloride ion has a 1− **charge.**

One magnesium ion and two chloride ions have an overall **charge of (2+) + 2(1−) = 0**

Figure 7 *The symbols on this music are understood around the world—just like chemical symbols!*

Chemical Equations

A composer writing a piece of music, like the one in **Figure 7,** must communicate to the musician what notes to play, how long to play each note, and in what style each note should be played. The composer does not use words to describe what must happen. Instead, he or she uses musical symbols to communicate in a way that can be easily understood by anyone in the world who can read music.

Similarly, people who work with chemical reactions need to communicate information about reactions clearly to other people throughout the world. Describing reactions using long descriptive sentences would require translations into other languages. Chemists have developed a method of describing reactions that is short and easily understood by anyone in the world who understands chemical formulas. A **chemical equation** is a shorthand description of a chemical reaction using chemical formulas and symbols. Because each element's chemical symbol is understood around the world, a chemical equation needs no translation.

Figure 8 *Charcoal is used to cook food on a barbecue. When carbon in charcoal reacts with oxygen in the air, the primary product is carbon dioxide.*

Reactants Yield Products Consider the example of carbon reacting with oxygen to yield carbon dioxide, as shown in **Figure 8.** The starting materials in a chemical reaction are **reactants** (ree AKT uhnts). The substances formed from a reaction are **products.** In this example, carbon and oxygen are reactants, and carbon dioxide is the product formed. The parts of the chemical equation for this reaction are described in **Figure 9.**

Figure 9 The Parts of a Chemical Equation

The formulas of the **reactants** are written before the arrow.

The formulas of the **products** are written after the arrow.

$$C + O_2 \rightarrow CO_2$$

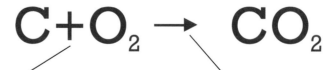

A **plus sign** separates the formulas of two or more reactants or products from one another.

The **arrow,** also called the yields sign, separates the formulas of the reactants from the formulas of the products.

Accuracy Is Important The symbol or formula for each substance in the reaction must be written correctly. For a compound, determine if it is covalent or ionic, and write the appropriate formula. For an element, use the proper chemical symbol, and be sure to use a subscript of 2 for the diatomic elements. (The seven diatomic elements are hydrogen, nitrogen, oxygen, fluorine, chlorine, bromine, and iodine.) An equation with an incorrect chemical symbol or formula will not accurately describe the reaction. In fact, even a simple mistake can make a huge difference, as shown in **Figure 10.**

Figure 10 *The symbols and formulas shown here are similar, but don't confuse them while writing an equation!*

The chemical formula for the compound carbon dioxide is **CO_2.** Carbon dioxide is a colorless, odorless gas that you exhale.

The chemical formula for the compound carbon monoxide is **CO.** Carbon monoxide is a colorless, odorless, poisonous gas.

The chemical symbol for the element cobalt is **Co.** Cobalt is a hard, bluish gray metal.

 Self-Check

When calcium bromide reacts with chlorine, bromine and calcium chloride are produced. Write an equation to describe this reaction. Identify each substance as either a reactant or a product. *(See page 136 to check your answers.)*

An Equation Must Be Balanced In a chemical reaction, every atom in the reactants becomes part of the products. Atoms are never lost or gained in a chemical reaction. When writing a chemical equation, you must show that the number of atoms of each element in the reactants equals the number of atoms of those elements in the products by writing a balanced equation.

MATH BREAK

Balancing Act

When balancing a chemical equation, you must place coefficients in front of an entire chemical formula, never in the middle of a formula. Notice where the coefficients are in the balanced equation below:

$$F_2 + 2KCl \longrightarrow 2KF + Cl_2$$

Now It's Your Turn

Write balanced equations for the following:

$$HCl + Na_2S \longrightarrow H_2S + NaCl$$
$$Al + Cl_2 \longrightarrow AlCl_3$$

How to Balance an Equation Writing a balanced equation requires the use of coefficients (кон uh FISH uhnts). A *coefficient* is a number placed in front of a chemical symbol or formula. When counting atoms, you multiply a coefficient by the subscript of each of the elements in the formula that follows it. Thus, $2CO_2$ represents 2 carbon dioxide molecules. Together the two molecules contain a total of 2 carbon atoms and 4 oxygen atoms. Coefficients are used when balancing equations because the subscripts in the formulas cannot be changed. Changing a subscript changes the formula so that it no longer represents the correct substance. Study **Figure 11** to see how to use coefficients to balance an equation. Then you can practice balancing equations by doing the MathBreak at left.

Figure 11 *Follow these steps to write a balanced equation for $H_2 + O_2 \longrightarrow H_2O$.*

1 **Count the atoms** of each element in the reactants and in the products. You can see that there are fewer oxygen atoms in the products than in the reactants.

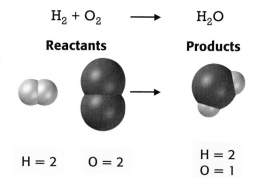

$$H_2 + O_2 \longrightarrow H_2O$$

Reactants   **Products**

H = 2   O = 2

H = 2
O = 1

2 **To balance the oxygen atoms,** place the coefficient *2* in front of water's formula. This gives you 2 oxygen atoms in both the reactants and the products. But now there are too few hydrogen atoms in the reactants.

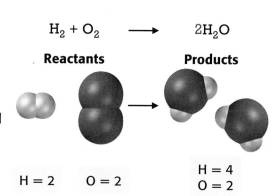

$$H_2 + O_2 \longrightarrow 2H_2O$$

Reactants   **Products**

H = 2   O = 2

H = 4
O = 2

3 **To balance the hydrogen atoms,** place the coefficient *2* in front of hydrogen's formula. But just to be sure your answer is correct, always double-check your work!

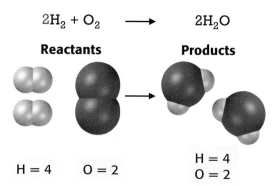

$$2H_2 + O_2 \longrightarrow 2H_2O$$

Reactants   **Products**

H = 4   O = 2

H = 4
O = 2

Become a better balancer of chemical equations on page 106 of the LabBook.

Mass Is Conserved—It's a Law! The practice of balancing equations is a result of the work of a French chemist, Antoine Lavoisier (luh vwa ZYAY). In the 1700s, Lavoisier performed experiments in which he carefully measured and compared the masses of the substances involved in chemical reactions. He determined that the total mass of the reactants equaled the total mass of the products. Lavoisier's work led to the **law of conservation of mass,** which states that mass is neither created nor destroyed in ordinary chemical and physical changes. Thus, a chemical equation must show the same number and kind of atom on both sides of the arrow. The law of conservation of mass is demonstrated in **Figure 12.** You can explore this law for yourself in the QuickLab at right.

Figure 12 In this demonstration, magnesium in the flash-bulb of a camera reacts with oxygen. Notice that the mass is the same before and after the reaction takes place.

 Quick Lab

Mass Conservation

1. Place 5 g (1 tsp) of **baking soda** into a **sealable plastic bag.**
2. Place 5 mL (1 tsp) of **vinegar** into a **plastic film canister.** Close the lid.
3. Use a **balance** to determine the masses of the bag with baking soda and the canister with vinegar, and record both values in your ScienceLog.
4. Place the canister into the bag. Squeeze the air out of the bag, and tightly seal it.
5. Open the canister in the bag. Mix the vinegar with the baking soda.
6. When the reaction has stopped, measure the total mass of the bag and its contents.
7. Compare the mass of the materials before and after the reaction.

SECTION REVIEW

1. List four clues that a chemical reaction is occurring.

2. How many atoms of each element make up $2Na_3PO_4$?

3. Write the chemical formulas for carbon tetrachloride and calcium bromide.

4. Explain how a balanced chemical equation illustrates that mass is never lost or gained in a chemical reaction.

5. **Applying Concepts** Write the balanced chemical equation for methane, CH_4, reacting with oxygen gas to produce water and carbon dioxide.

internet connect

 SC*LINKS*
NSTA

TOPIC: Chemical Formulas, Chemical Equations
GO TO: www.scilinks.org
*sci*LINKS **NUMBER:** HSTP335, HSTP340

Terms to Learn

synthesis reaction
decomposition reaction
single-replacement reaction
double-replacement reaction

What You'll Do

◆ Describe four types of chemical reactions.
◆ Classify a chemical equation as one of the four types of chemical reactions described here.

Types of Chemical Reactions

Imagine having to learn 50 chemical reactions. Sound tough? Well, there are thousands of known chemical reactions. It would be impossible to remember them all. But there is help! Remember that the elements are divided into categories based on their properties. In a similar way, reactions can be classified according to their similarities.

Many reactions can be grouped into one of four categories: synthesis (SIN thuh sis), decomposition, single replacement, and double replacement. By dividing reactions into these categories, you can better understand the patterns of how reactants become products. As you learn about each type of reaction, study the models provided to help you recognize each type of reaction.

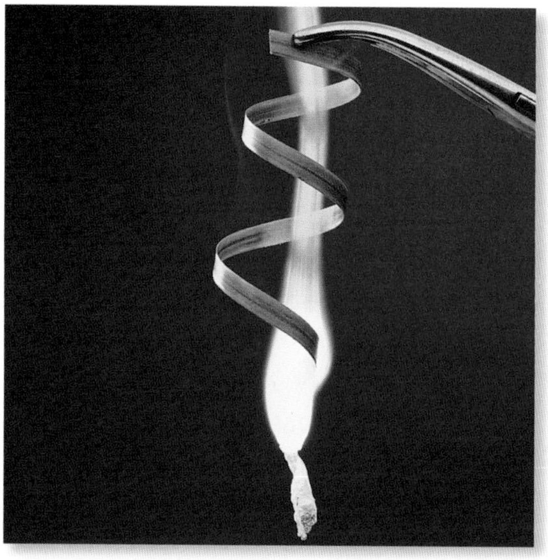

Synthesis Reactions

A **synthesis reaction** is a reaction in which two or more substances combine to form a single compound. For example, the synthesis reaction in which the compound magnesium oxide is produced is seen in **Figure 13.** (This is the same reaction that occurs in the flashbulb in Figure 12.) One way to remember what happens in each type of reaction is to imagine people at a dance. A synthesis reaction would be modeled by two people joining to form a dancing couple, as shown in **Figure 14.**

Figure 13 *The synthesis reaction that occurs when magnesium reacts with oxygen in the air forms the compound magnesium oxide.*

Figure 14 *A model for the synthesis reaction of sodium reacting with chlorine to form sodium chloride is shown below.*

$$2Na + Cl_2 \longrightarrow 2NaCl$$

Decomposition Reactions

A **decomposition reaction** is a reaction in which a single compound breaks down to form two or more simpler substances. The decomposition of water is shown in **Figure 15.** Decomposition is the reverse of synthesis. The dance model would represent a decomposition reaction as a dancing couple splitting up, as shown in **Figure 16.**

Figure 15 *Water can be decomposed into the elements hydrogen and oxygen through electrolysis.*

Figure 16 *A model for the decomposition reaction of carbonic acid to form water and carbon dioxide is shown below.*

$$H_2CO_3 \longrightarrow H_2O + CO_2$$

Single-Replacement Reactions

A **single-replacement reaction** is a reaction in which an element takes the place of another element that is part of a compound. The products of single-replacement reactions are a new compound and a different element. The dance model for single-replacement reactions is a person who cuts in on a couple dancing. A new couple is formed and a different person is left alone, as shown in **Figure 17.**

Figure 17 *A model for a single-replacement reaction of zinc reacting with hydrochloric acid to form zinc chloride and hydrogen is shown below.*

$$Zn + 2HCl \longrightarrow ZnCl_2 + H_2$$

Some Elements Are More Reactive Than Others In a single-replacement reaction, a more-reactive element can replace a less-reactive one from a compound. However, the opposite reaction does not occur, as shown in **Figure 18.**

Figure 18 *More-reactive elements replace less-reactive elements in single-replacement reactions.*

$$Cu + 2AgNO_3 \rightarrow 2Ag + Cu(NO_3)_2$$
Copper is more reactive than silver.

$$Ag + Cu(NO_3)_2 \rightarrow \text{No reaction}$$
Silver is less reactive than copper.

Double-Replacement Reactions

Figure 19 *A model for the double-replacement reaction of sodium chloride reacting with silver fluoride to form sodium fluoride and the precipitate silver chloride is shown below.*

A **double-replacement reaction** is a reaction in which ions in two compounds switch places. One of the products of this reaction is often a gas or a precipitate. A double-replacement reaction in the dance model would be two couples dancing and switching partners, as shown in **Figure 19.**

$$NaCl + AgF \longrightarrow NaF + AgCl$$

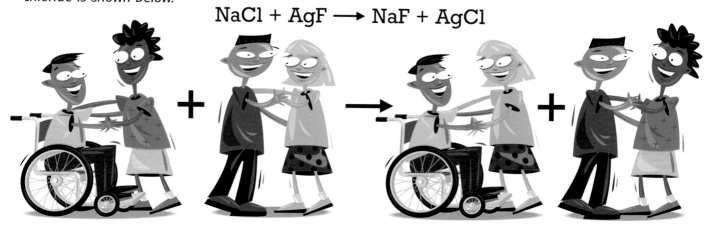

internet**connect**

SC*i*LINKS.
NSTA

TOPIC: Reaction Types
GO TO: www.scilinks.org
*sci***LINKS NUMBER:** HSTP343

SECTION REVIEW

1. What type of reaction does each of the following equations represent?

   a. $FeS + 2HCl \longrightarrow FeCl_2 + H_2S$

   b. $NH_4OH \longrightarrow NH_3 + H_2O$

2. Which type of reaction always has an element and a compound as reactants?

3. **Comparing Concepts** Compare synthesis and decomposition reactions.

Terms to Learn

exothermic
endothermic
law of conservation of energy
activation energy
catalyst
inhibitor

What You'll Do

◆ Compare exothermic and endothermic reactions.
◆ Explain activation energy.
◆ Interpret an energy diagram.
◆ Describe the factors that affect the rate of a reaction.

Energy and Rates of Chemical Reactions

You just learned one method of classifying chemical reactions. In this section, you will learn how to classify reactions in terms of the energy associated with the reaction and learn how to change the rate at which the reaction occurs.

Every Reaction Involves Energy

All chemical reactions involve chemical energy. Remember that during a reaction, chemical bonds in the reactants break as they absorb energy. As new bonds form in the products, energy is released. Energy is released or absorbed in the overall reaction depending on how the chemical energy of the reactants compares with the chemical energy of the products.

Energy Is Released in Exothermic Reactions If the chemical energy of the reactants is greater than the chemical energy of the products, the difference in energy is released during the reaction. A chemical reaction in which energy is released or removed is called **exothermic.** *Exo* means "go out" or "exit," and *thermic* means "heat" or "energy." The energy can be released in several different forms, as shown in **Figure 20.** The energy released in an exothermic reaction is often written as a product in a chemical equation, as in this equation:

$$2Na + Cl_2 \longrightarrow 2NaCl + energy$$

Figure 20 Types of Energy Released in Reactions

Light energy is released in the exothermic reaction taking place in these light sticks.

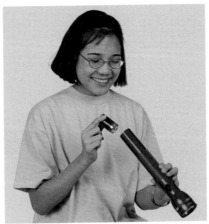

Electrical energy is released in the exothermic reaction taking place in the dry cells in this flashlight.

Light and thermal energy are released in the exothermic reaction taking place in this campfire.

Biology CONNECTION

Photosynthesis is an endothermic process in which light energy from the sun is used to produce glucose, a simple sugar. The equation that describes photosynthesis is as follows:

$$6CO_2 + 6H_2O + energy \longrightarrow C_6H_{12}O_6 + 6O_2$$

The cells in your body use glucose to get the energy they need through cellular respiration, an exothermic process described by the reverse of the above reaction:

$$C_6H_{12}O_6 + 6O_2 \longrightarrow 6CO_2 + 6H_2O + energy$$

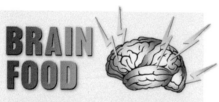

Energy Is Absorbed in Endothermic Reactions If the chemical energy of the reactants is less than the chemical energy of the products, the difference in energy is absorbed during the reaction. A chemical reaction in which energy is absorbed is called **endothermic.** *Endo* means "go in," and *thermic* means "heat" or "energy." The energy absorbed in an endothermic reaction is often written as a reactant in a chemical equation, as in this equation:

$$2H_2O + energy \longrightarrow 2H_2 + O_2$$

Energy Is Conserved—It's a Law! You learned that mass is never created or destroyed in chemical reactions. The same holds true for energy. The **law of conservation of energy** states that energy can be neither created nor destroyed. The energy released in exothermic reactions was originally stored in the reactants. And the energy absorbed in endothermic reactions does not just vanish. It is stored in the products that form. If you could carefully measure all the energy in a reaction, you would find that the total amount of energy (of all types) is the same before and after the reaction.

Activation Energy Gets a Reaction Started A match can be used to light a campfire—but only if the match is lit! A strike-anywhere match, like the one shown in **Figure 21,** has all the reactants it needs to be able to burn. And though the chemicals on a match are intended to react and burn, they will not ignite by themselves. Energy is needed to start the reaction. The minimum amount of energy needed for substances to react is called **activation energy.**

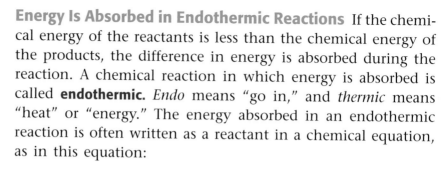

Figure 21 *Rubbing the tip of this strike-anywhere match on a rough surface provides the energy needed to get the chemicals to react.*

The friction of striking a match heats the substances on the match, breaking bonds in the reactants and allowing the new bonds in the products to form. Chemical reactions require some energy to get started. An electric spark in a car's engine provides activation energy to begin the burning of gasoline. Light can also provide the activation energy for a reaction. You can better understand activation energy and the differences between exothermic reactions and endothermic reactions by studying the diagrams in **Figure 22.**

Figure 22 Energy Diagrams

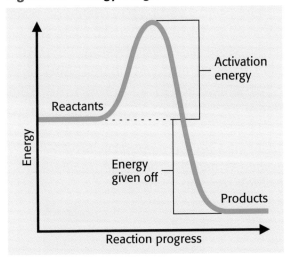

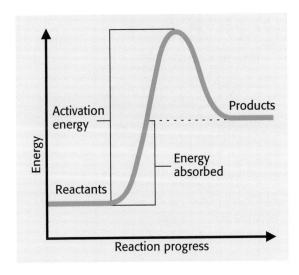

Exothermic Reaction Once begun, an exothermic reaction can continue to occur, as in a fire. The energy released as the product forms continues to supply the activation energy needed for the substances to react.

Endothermic Reaction An endothermic reaction requires a continuous supply of energy. Energy must be absorbed to provide the activation energy needed for the substances to react.

Fresh Hydrogen Peroxide

Hydrogen peroxide is used as a disinfectant for minor scrapes and cuts because it decomposes to produce oxygen gas and water, which help cleanse the wound. The decomposition of hydrogen peroxide is an exothermic reaction. Explain why hydrogen peroxide must be stored in a dark bottle to maintain its freshness. (HINT: What type of energy would be blocked by this type of container?)

Factors Affecting Rates of Reactions

You can think of a reaction as occurring only if the particles of reactants collide when they have enough energy to break the appropriate bonds. The rate of a reaction is a measure of how rapidly the reaction takes place. Four factors that affect the rate of a reaction are temperature, concentration, surface area, and the presence of a catalyst or inhibitor.

Fighting fires with slime? Read more about it on page 50.

Temperature An increase in temperature increases the rate of a reaction. At higher temperatures, particles of reactants move faster, so they collide with each other more frequently and with more energy. More particles therefore have the activation energy needed to react and can change into products faster. Thus, more particles react in a shorter time. You can see this effect in **Figure 23** and by doing the QuickLab at left.

Figure 23 *The light stick on the right glows brighter than the one on the left because the higher temperature causes the rate of the reaction to increase.*

Concentration Generally, increasing the concentration of reactants increases the rate of a reaction, as shown in **Figure 24.** *Concentration* is a measure of the amount of one substance dissolved in another. Increasing the concentration increases the number of reactant particles present and decreases the distance between them. The reactant particles collide more often, so more particles react each second. Increasing the concentration is similar to having more people in a room. The more people that are in the room, the more frequently they will collide and interact.

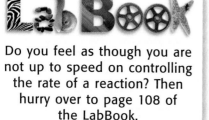

Do you feel as though you are not up to speed on controlling the rate of a reaction? Then hurry over to page 108 of the LabBook.

Figure 24 *The reaction on the right produces bubbles of hydrogen gas at a faster rate because the concentration of hydrochloric acid used is higher.*

Surface Area Increasing the surface area, or the amount of exposed surface, of solid reactants increases the rate of a reaction. Grinding a solid into a powder exposes more particles of the reactant to other reactant particles. The number of collisions between reactant particles increases, increasing the rate of the reaction. You can see the effect of increasing the surface area in the QuickLab at right.

Catalysts and Inhibitors Some reactions would be too slow to be useful without a catalyst (KAT uh LIST). A **catalyst** is a substance that speeds up a reaction without being permanently changed. A catalyst lowers the activation energy of a reaction, which allows the reaction to occur more rapidly. Most reactions in your body are sped up using catalysts called enzymes. Catalysts are even found in cars, as seen in **Figure 25.**

An **inhibitor** is a substance that slows down or stops a chemical reaction. Preservatives added to foods are inhibitors that slow down reactions in the bacteria or fungus that can spoil food. Many poisons are also inhibitors.

Figure 25 *This catalytic converter contains platinum and palladium—two catalysts that increase the rate of reactions that make the car's exhaust less polluting.*

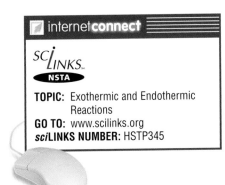

QuickLab

I'm Crushed!

1. Fill **two clear plastic cups** half-full with **room-temperature water.**

2. Fold a **sheet of paper** around one-quarter of an **effervescent tablet.** Carefully crush the tablet.

3. Get another one-quarter of an effervescent tablet. Carefully pour the crushed tablet into one cup, and place the uncrushed tablet in the second cup.

4. Observe the reaction, and record your observations in your ScienceLog.

5. In which cup did the reaction occur at a greater rate? What evidence supports your answer?

6. Explain why the water in each cup must have the same temperature.

SECTION REVIEW

1. What is activation energy?

2. List four ways to increase the rate of a reaction.

3. **Comparing Concepts** Compare exothermic and endothermic reactions.

4. **Interpreting Graphics** Does this energy diagram show an exothermic or an endothermic reaction? How can you tell?

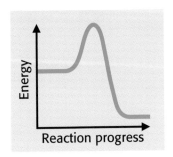

internet**connect**

SCiLINKS
NSTA

TOPIC: Exothermic and Endothermic Reactions
GO TO: www.scilinks.org
sciLINKS NUMBER: HSTP345

Putting Elements Together

You have learned that the products of a chemical reaction have chemical and physical properties different from the reactants. In this activity, you will observe the reaction between copper and oxygen to form copper(II) oxide.

MATERIALS

- metric balance
- evaporating dish
- weighing paper
- copper powder
- ring stand and ring
- wire gauze
- Bunsen burner or portable burner
- spark igniter
- tongs

Procedure

1 Copy the table shown on the next page into your ScienceLog, or create a similar one on a computer.

2 Use the metric balance to measure the mass (to the nearest 0.1 g) of the empty evaporating dish. Record this mass in the table.

3 Using weighing paper, measure approximately 10 g of copper powder. Record the mass (to the nearest 0.1 g) in the table.
Caution: Wear goggles, an apron, and protective gloves when working with copper powder.

4 Use the weighing paper to place the copper powder in the evaporating dish. Spread the powder over the bottom and the sides as much as possible. Throw away the weighing paper.

5 Set up the ring stand and ring. Place the wire gauze on top of the ring. Carefully place the evaporating dish on the wire gauze.

6 Place the Bunsen burner under the ring and wire gauze. Use the spark igniter to light the Bunsen burner. Heat the evaporating dish for 10 minutes.
Caution: Use extreme care when working near an open flame.

7 Turn off the burner, and allow the evaporating dish to cool for 10 minutes. Use tongs to remove the evaporating dish, and place it on the balance to find the mass. Record the mass in the table.

Data Collection Table	
Object	**Mass (g)**
Evaporating dish	
Copper powder	
Copper + evaporating dish after heating	
Copper(II) oxide	

DO NOT WRITE IN BOOK

8 Find the mass of the reaction product—copper(II) oxide—by subtracting the mass of the evaporating dish from the combined mass of the evaporating dish and copper powder after heating. Record this mass in the table.

Analysis

9 What evidence of a chemical reaction did you observe after the copper was heated?

10 Explain why there was a change in mass.

11 Why was powdered copper used rather than a small piece of copper? (Hint: How does surface area affect the rate of the reaction?)

12 Why was the copper heated? (Hint: Look in your book for the discussion of activation energy.)

13 The copper bottoms of cooking pots can turn black when used. How is that similar to the results you got in this lab?

Chapter Highlights

SECTION 1

Vocabulary

chemical reaction *(p. 28)*

chemical formula *(p. 30)*

chemical equation *(p. 32)*

reactants *(p. 32)*

products *(p. 32)*

law of conservation of mass *(p. 35)*

Section Notes

- Chemical reactions form new substances with different properties than the starting substances.

- Clues that a chemical reaction is taking place include formation of a gas or solid, a color change, and an energy change.

- A chemical formula tells the composition of a compound using chemical symbols and subscripts. Subscripts are small numbers written below and to the right of a symbol in a formula.

- Chemical formulas can sometimes be written from the names of covalent compounds and ionic compounds.

- A chemical equation describes a reaction using formulas, symbols, and coefficients.

- A balanced equation uses coefficients to illustrate the law of conservation of mass, that mass is neither created nor destroyed during a chemical reaction.

Labs

Finding a Balance *(p. 106)*

SECTION 2

Vocabulary

synthesis reaction *(p. 36)*

decomposition reaction *(p. 37)*

single-replacement reaction *(p. 37)*

double-replacement reaction *(p. 38)*

Section Notes

- Many chemical reactions can be classified as one of four types by comparing reactants with products.

- In synthesis reactions, the reactants form a single product.

- In decomposition reactions, a single reactant breaks apart into two or more simpler products.

☑ Skills Check

Math Concepts

SUBSCRIPTS AND COEFFICIENTS   A subscript is a number written below and to the right of a chemical symbol when writing the chemical formula of a compound. A coefficient is a number written in front of a chemical formula in a chemical equation. When you balance a chemical equation, you cannot change the subscripts in a formula; you can only add coefficients, as seen in the equation $2H_2 + O_2 \longrightarrow 2H_2O$.

Visual Understanding

REACTION TYPES   It can be challenging to identify which type of reaction a particular chemical equation represents. Review four reaction types by studying Figures 14, 16, 17, and 19.

- In single-replacement reactions, a more-reactive element takes the place of a less-reactive element in a compound. No reaction will occur if a less-reactive element is placed with a compound containing a more-reactive element.

- In double-replacement reactions, ions in two compounds switch places. A gas or precipitate is often formed.

Labs

Putting Elements Together (p. 44–45)

Vocabulary

exothermic (p. 39)

endothermic (p. 40)

law of conservation of energy (p. 40)

activation energy (p. 40)

catalyst (p. 43)

inhibitor (p. 43)

Section Notes

- Energy is released in exothermic reactions. The energy released can be written as a product in a chemical equation.

- Energy is absorbed in endothermic reactions. The energy absorbed can be written as a reactant in a chemical equation.

- The law of conservation of energy states that energy is neither created nor destroyed.

- Activation energy is the energy needed to start a chemical reaction.

- Energy diagrams indicate whether a reaction is exothermic or endothermic by showing whether energy is given off or absorbed during the reaction.

- The rate of a chemical reaction is affected by temperature, concentration, surface area, and the presence of a catalyst or inhibitor.

- Raising the temperature, increasing the concentration, increasing the surface area, and adding a catalyst can increase the rate of a reaction.

Labs

Cata-what? Catalyst! (p. 107)

Speed Control (p. 108)

---

internetconnect

GO TO: go.hrw.com

Visit the **HRW** Web site for a variety of learning tools related to this chapter. Just type in the keyword:

KEYWORD: HSTREA

*SCiLINKS*sm

N S T A

GO TO: www.scilinks.org

Visit the **National Science Teachers Association** on-line Web site for Internet resources related to this chapter. Just type in the *sci*LINKS number for more information about the topic:

TOPIC: Chemical Reactions	*sci*LINKS NUMBER: HSTP330
TOPIC: Chemical Formulas	*sci*LINKS NUMBER: HSTP335
TOPIC: Chemical Equations	*sci*LINKS NUMBER: HSTP340
TOPIC: Reaction Types	*sci*LINKS NUMBER: HSTP343
TOPIC: Exothermic and Endothermic Reactions	*sci*LINKS NUMBER: HSTP345

Chapter Review

To complete the following sentences, choose the correct term from each pair of terms listed below.

1. Adding a(n) ____ will slow down a chemical reaction. (*catalyst* or *inhibitor*)

2. A chemical reaction that gives off light is called ____. (*exothermic* or *endothermic*)

3. A chemical reaction that forms one compound from two or more substances is called a ____. (*synthesis reaction* or *decomposition reaction*)

4. The *2* in the formula Ag_2S is a ____. (*subscript* or *coefficient*)

5. The starting materials in a chemical reaction are ____. (*reactants* or *products*)

UNDERSTANDING CONCEPTS

Multiple Choice

6. Balancing a chemical equation so that the same number of atoms of each element is found in both the reactants and the products is an illustration of
   a. activation energy.
   b. the law of conservation of energy.
   c. the law of conservation of mass.
   d. a double-replacement reaction.

7. What is the correct chemical formula for calcium chloride?
   a. CaCl   c. Ca_2Cl
   b. $CaCl_2$ d. Ca_2Cl_2

8. In which type of reaction do ions in two compounds switch places?
   a. synthesis
   b. decomposition
   c. single-replacement
   d. double-replacement

9. Which is an example of the use of activation energy?
   a. plugging in an iron
   b. playing basketball
   c. holding a lit match to paper
   d. eating

10. Enzymes in your body act as catalysts. Thus, the role of enzymes is to
    a. increase the rate of chemical reactions.
    b. decrease the rate of chemical reactions.
    c. help you breathe.
    d. inhibit chemical reactions.

Short Answer

11. Classify each of the following reactions:
    a. $Fe + O_2 \longrightarrow Fe_2O_3$
    b. $Al + CuSO_4 \longrightarrow Al_2(SO_4)_3 + Cu$
    c. $Ba(CN)_2 + H_2SO_4 \longrightarrow BaSO_4 + HCN$

12. Name two ways that you could increase the rate of a chemical reaction.

13. Acetic acid, a compound found in vinegar, reacts with baking soda to produce carbon dioxide, water, and sodium acetate. Without writing an equation, identify the reactants and the products of this reaction.

Concept Mapping

14. Use the following terms to create a concept map: chemical reaction, chemical equation, chemical formulas, reactants, products, coefficients, subscripts.

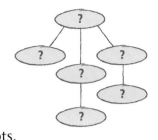

CRITICAL THINKING AND PROBLEM SOLVING

15. Your friend is very worried by rumors he has heard about a substance called dihydrogen monoxide. What could you say to your friend to calm his fears? (Be sure to write the formula of the substance.)

16. As long as proper safety precautions have been taken, why can explosives be transported long distances without exploding?

MATH IN SCIENCE

17. Calculate the number of atoms of each element shown in each of the following:
a. $CaSO_4$
b. $4NaOCl$
c. $Fe(NO_3)_2$
d. $2Al_2(CO_3)_3$

18. Write balanced equations for the following:
a. $Fe + O_2 \longrightarrow Fe_2O_3$
b. $Al + CuSO_4 \longrightarrow Al_2(SO_4)_3 + Cu$
c. $Ba(CN)_2 + H_2SO_4 \longrightarrow BaSO_4 + HCN$

19. Write and balance chemical equations from each of the following descriptions:
a. Bromine reacts with sodium iodide to form iodine and sodium bromide.
b. Phosphorus reacts with oxygen gas to form diphosphorus pentoxide.
c. Lithium oxide decomposes to form lithium and oxygen.

INTERPRETING GRAPHICS

20. What evidence in the photo supports the claim that a chemical reaction is taking place?

21. Use the energy diagram below to answer the questions that follow.

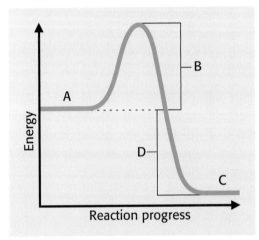

a. Which letter represents the energy of the products?
b. Which letter represents the activation energy of the reaction?
c. Is energy given off or absorbed by this reaction?

Reading Check-up Take a minute to review your answers to the Pre-Reading Questions found at the bottom of page 26. Have your answers changed? If necessary, revise your answers based on what you have learned since you began this chapter.

EYE ON THE ENVIRONMENT

Slime That Fire!

Once a fire starts in the hard-to-reach mountains of the western United States, it is difficult to stop. Trees, grasses, and brush can provide an overwhelming supply of fuel. In order to stop a fire, firefighters make a fire line. This is an area where all the burnable materials are removed from the ground. How would you slow down a fire to give a ground crew more time to build a fire line? Would you suggest dropping water from a plane? That is not a bad idea, but what if you had something even better than water—like some slimy red goop?

Red Goop Goes the Distance

The slimy red goop is actually a powerful fire retardant. The goop is a mixture of a powder and water that is loaded directly onto an old military plane. Carrying between 4,500 and 11,000 L of the slime, the plane drops it all in front of the raging flames when the pilot presses the button.

The amount of water added to the powder depends on the location of the fire. If a fire is burning over shrubs and grasses, more water is needed. In this form the goop actually rains down to the ground through the treetops. But if a fire is burning in tall trees, less water is used so the slime will glob onto the branches and ooze down very slowly.

Failed Flames

The burning of trees, grass, and brush is an exothermic reaction. A fire retardant slows or stops this self-feeding reaction. A fire retardant increases the activation energy for the materials it is applied to. Although a lot depends on how hot the fire is when it hits the area treated with the retardant and how much of the retardant

▲ *This plane is dropping fire retardant on a forest fire.*

is applied, firefighters on the ground can gain valuable time when a fire is slowed with a fire retardant. This extra time allows them to create a fire line that will ultimately stop the fire.

Neon Isn't Necessary

Once a fire is put out, the slimy red streaks left on the blackened ground can be an eyesore. To solve the problem, scientists have created special dyes for the retardant. These dyes make the goop neon colors when it is first applied, but after a few days in the sun, the goop turns a natural brown shade!

What Do They Study?

▶ Do some research to learn about a firefighter's training. What classes and exams are firefighters required to pass? How do they maintain their certifications once they become firefighters?

CAREERS

ARSON INVESTIGATOR

Once a fire dies down, you might see arson investigator **Lt. Larry McKee** on the scene. "After the fire is out, I can investigate the fire scene to determine where the fire started and how it started. If it was intentionally set and I'm successful at putting the arson case together, I can get a conviction. That's very satisfying," says Lt. McKee.

During a fire, fuel and oxygen combine in a chemical reaction called combustion. On the scene, Lt. Larry McKee questions witnesses and firefighters about what they saw. He knows, for example, that the color of the smoke can indicate certain chemicals.

McKee explains that fires usually burn "up and out, in a V shape." To find where the V begins, he says, "We work from the area with the least amount of damage to the one with the most damage. This normally leads us to the point of origin." Once the origin has been determined, it's time to call in the dogs!

An Accelerant-Sniffing Canine

"We have what we call an accelerant-sniffing canine. Our canine, Nikki, has been trained to detect approximately 11 different chemicals." When Nikki arrives on the scene, she sniffs for traces of chemicals, called accelerants, that may have been used to start the fire. When she finds one, she immediately starts to dig at it. At that point, McKee takes a sample from the area and sends it to the lab for analysis.

At the Lab

Once at the laboratory, the sample is treated so that any accelerants in it are dissolved in a liquid. A small amount of the liquid is then injected into an instrument called a *gas chromatograph.* The instrument heats the liquid, forming a mixture of gases. The gases then are passed through a flame. As each gas passes through the flame, it "causes a fluctuation in an electronic signal, which creates our graphs."

Solving the Case

If the laboratory report indicates that a suspicious accelerant has been found, McKee begins to search for arson suspects. By combining detective work with scientific evidence, fire investigators can successfully catch and convict arsonists.

Fascinating Fire Facts

▶ The temperature of a house fire can reach 980°C! At that temperature, aluminum window frames melt, and furniture goes up in flames. Do some research to discover three more facts about fires. Create a display with two or more classmates to illustrate some of your facts.

▲ *Nikki searches for traces of gasoline, kerosene, and other accelerants.*

Chemical Compounds

Pre-Reading Questions

1. What is the difference between ionic compounds and covalent compounds?

2. What is an acid?

3. What is a hydrocarbon?

SOMETHING'S FISHY

Some people keep saltwater aquariums as a hobby. The living organisms in these aquariums—fish, coral, and algae—must have the correct environment, or they might die. Many things must be controlled in the aquarium. For example, the pH of the water must stay within a certain range. The amount of salt and other compounds in the water also must be within a certain range. In this chapter, you will learn about pH. You will also learn about salts and other chemical compounds.

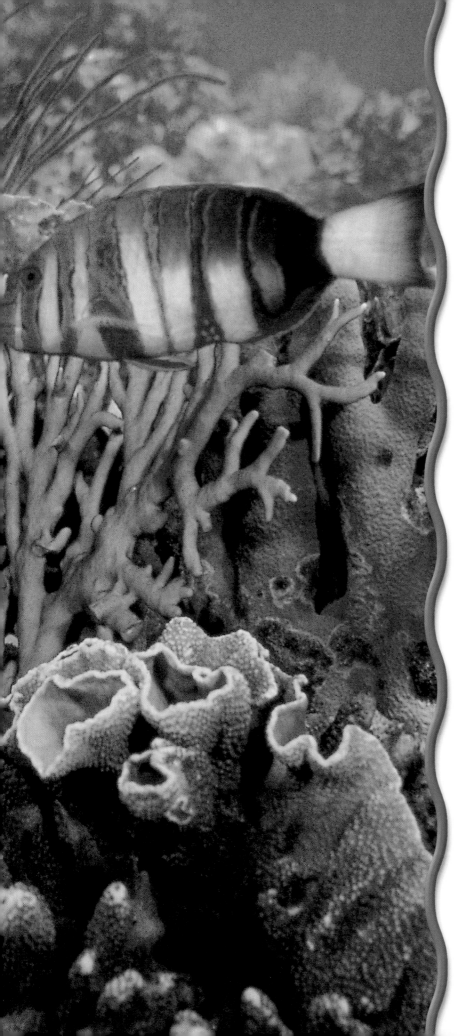

STICKING TOGETHER

In this activity you will demonstrate the force that keeps particles together in some compounds.

Procedure

1. Blow up **two balloons.** Rub them with a piece of **wool cloth.**

2. Hold the balloons by their necks. Move the balloons near each other. Describe in your ScienceLog what you see.

3. Put one of the balloons against a wall. Record your observations in your ScienceLog.

Analysis

4. The balloons are charged by rubbing them with the wool cloth. Like charges repel each other. Opposite charges attract each other. Infer whether the balloons have like or opposite charges. Explain your answer.

5. The two types of charge are negative and positive. The balloon in step 3 has a negative charge. Infer what the charge is on the wall where you put the balloon. Explain.

6. The particles that make up some compounds are attracted to each other in the same way that the balloon is attracted to the wall. What can you infer about the particles that make up such compounds?

Terms to Learn

ionic compounds
covalent compounds

What You'll Do

◆ Describe the properties of ionic and covalent compounds.

◆ Classify compounds as ionic or covalent based on their properties.

Ionic and Covalent Compounds

The world around you is made up of chemical compounds. Chemical compounds are pure substances composed of ions or molecules. There are millions of different kinds of compounds, so you can imagine how classifying them might be helpful. One simple way to classify compounds is by grouping them according to the type of bond they contain.

Ionic Compounds

Compounds that contain ionic bonds are called **ionic compounds.** Remember that an ionic bond is the force of attraction between two oppositely charged ions. Ionic compounds can be formed by the reaction of a metal with a nonmetal. Electrons are transferred from the metal atoms (which become positively charged ions) to the nonmetal atoms (which become negatively charged ions). For example, when sodium reacts with chlorine, as shown in **Figure 1,** the ionic compound sodium chloride, or ordinary table salt, is formed.

Figure 1 *An ionic compound is formed when the metal sodium reacts with the nonmetal chlorine. Sodium chloride is formed in the reaction, and energy is released as light and thermal energy.*

Brittleness The forces acting between the ions that make up ionic compounds give these compounds certain properties. Ionic compounds tend to be brittle, as shown in **Figure 2.** The ions that make up an ionic compound are arranged in a repeating three-dimensional pattern called a crystal lattice. The ions that make up the crystal lattice are arranged as alternating positive and negative ions. Each ion in the lattice is surrounded by ions of the opposite charge, and each ion is bonded to the ions around it. When an ionic compound is struck with a hammer, the pattern of ions in the crystal lattice is shifted. Ions with the same charge line up and repel one another, causing the crystal to shatter.

Figure 2 *Ionic compounds will shatter when hit with a hammer.*

High Melting Points Ionic compounds are almost always solid at room temperature, as shown in **Figure 3.** An ionic compound will melt only at temperatures high enough to overcome the strong ionic bonds between the ions. Sodium chloride, for instance, must be heated to 801°C before it will melt. This temperature is much higher than you can produce in your kitchen or even your school laboratory.

Magnesium oxide melts at 2,800°C.

Potassium dichromate melts at 398°C.

Nickel(II) oxide melts at 1,984°C.

Solubility and Electrical Conductivity Many ionic compounds dissolve easily in water. Molecules of water attract each of the ions of an ionic compound and pull them away from one another. The solution created when an ionic compound dissolves in water can conduct an electric current, as shown in **Figure 4.** The ions are able to move past one another and conduct the electric current in the solution. Keep in mind that an undissolved crystal of an ionic compound does not conduct an electric current.

Figure 3 *Each of these ionic compounds has a high melting point and is solid at room temperature.*

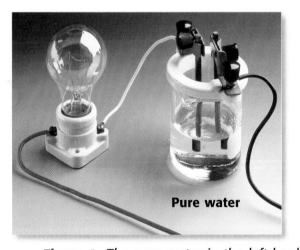

Pure water

Salt water

Figure 4 *The pure water in the left beaker does not conduct an electric current. The solution of salt water in the right beaker conducts an electric current, and the bulb lights up.*

Covalent Compounds

Compounds composed of elements that are covalently bonded are called **covalent compounds.** Remember that covalent bonds form when atoms share electrons. Gasoline, carbon dioxide, water, and sugar are well-known examples of covalent compounds.

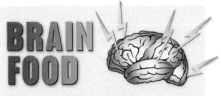

BRAIN FOOD

Molecules of covalent compounds can have anywhere from two atoms to hundreds or thousands of atoms! Small, lightweight molecules, like water or carbon dioxide, tend to form liquids or gases at room temperature. Heavier molecules, such as sugar or plastics, tend to form solids at room temperature.

Low Melting Points Covalent compounds exist as independent particles called molecules. The forces of attraction between molecules of covalent compounds are much weaker than the bonds between ions in a crystal lattice. Thus, covalent compounds have lower melting points than ionic compounds.

Solubility and Electrical Conductivity You have probably heard the phrase "oil and water don't mix." Oil, such as that used in salad dressing, is composed of covalent compounds. Many covalent compounds do not dissolve well in water. Water molecules have a stronger attraction for one another than they have for the molecules of most other covalent compounds. Thus, the molecules of the covalent compound get squeezed out as the water molecules pull together. Some covalent compounds do dissolve in water. Most of these solutions contain uncharged molecules dissolved in water and do not conduct an electric current, as shown in **Figure 5.** Some covalent compounds form ions when they dissolve in water. Solutions of these compounds, including compounds called acids, do conduct an electric current. You will learn more about acids in the next section.

Figure 5 *This solution of sugar, a covalent compound, in water does not conduct an electric current because the individual molecules of sugar are not charged.*

Sugar water

internetconnect

SCiLINKS.
NSTA

TOPIC: Ionic Compounds, Covalent Compounds
GO TO: www.scilinks.org
*sci*LINKS NUMBER: HSTP355, HSTP360

SECTION REVIEW

1. List two properties of ionic compounds.

2. List two properties of covalent compounds.

3. Methane is a gas at room temperature. What type of compound is this most likely to be?

4. **Comparing Concepts** Compare ionic and covalent compounds based on the type of particle that makes up each.

Terms to Learn

acid   pH
base   salt

What You'll Do

◆ Describe the properties and uses of acids and bases.
◆ Explain the difference between strong acids and bases and weak acids and bases.
◆ Identify acids and bases using the pH scale.
◆ Describe the properties and uses of salts.

Acids, Bases, and Salts

Have you ever noticed that when you squeeze lemon juice into tea, the color of the tea becomes lighter? Shown in **Figure 6,** lemon juice contains a substance called an acid that changes the color of a substance in the tea. The ability to change the color of certain chemicals is one property used to classify substances as acids or bases. A third category of substances, called salts, are formed by the reaction of an acid with a base.

Figure 6 *Acids, like those found in lemon juice, can change the color of tea.*

NEVER touch or taste a concentrated solution of a strong acid.

Acids

An **acid** is any compound that increases the number of hydrogen ions when dissolved in water, and whose solution tastes sour and can change the color of certain compounds.

Properties of Acids If you have ever had orange juice, you have experienced the sour taste of an acid. The taste of lemons, limes, and other citrus fruits is a result of citric acid. Taste, however, should NEVER be used as a test to identify an unknown chemical. Many acids are *corrosive,* meaning they destroy body tissue and clothing, and many are also poisonous.

Acids react with some metals to produce hydrogen gas, as shown in **Figure 7.** Adding an acid to baking soda or limestone produces a different gas, carbon dioxide.

Solutions of acids conduct an electric current because acids break apart to form ions in water. Acids increase the number of hydrogen ions, H^+, in a solution. However, the hydrogen ion does not normally exist alone. In a water solution, each hydrogen ion bonds to a water molecule, H_2O, to form a hydronium ion, H_3O^+.

Figure 7 *Bubbles of hydrogen gas are produced when zinc metal reacts with hydrochloric acid.*

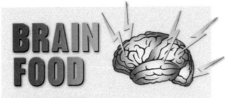

Detecting Acids As mentioned earlier, a property of acids is their ability to change the color of a substance. An *indicator* is a substance that changes color in the presence of an acid or base. An indicator commonly used is litmus. Paper strips containing litmus are available in both blue and red. When an acid is added to blue litmus paper, the color of the litmus changes to red, as shown in **Figure 8.** (Red litmus paper is used to detect bases, as will be discussed shortly.) Many plant materials, such as red cabbage, contain compounds that are indicators.

Figure 8 *Vinegar turns blue litmus paper red because it contains acetic acid.*

Figure 9 *The label on this car battery warns you that sulfuric acid is found in the battery.*

Uses of Acids Acids are used in many areas of industry as well as in your home. Sulfuric acid is the most widely produced industrial chemical in the world. It is used in the production of metals, paper, paint, detergents, and fertilizers. It is also used in car batteries, as shown in **Figure 9.** Nitric acid is used to make fertilizers, rubber, and plastics. Hydrochloric acid is used in the production of metals and to help keep swimming pools free of algae. It is also found in your stomach, where it aids in digestion. Citric acid and ascorbic acid (vitamin C) are found in orange juice, while carbonic acid and phosphoric acid help give extra "bite" to soft drinks.

Strong Versus Weak As an acid dissolves in water, its molecules break apart and produce hydrogen ions. When all the molecules of an acid break apart in water to produce hydrogen ions, the acid is considered a strong acid. Strong acids include sulfuric acid, nitric acid, and hydrochloric acid.

When few molecules of an acid break apart in water to produce hydrogen ions, the acid is considered a weak acid. Acetic acid, citric acid, carbonic acid, and phosphoric acid are all weak acids.

Bases

A **base** is any compound that increases the number of hydroxide ions when dissolved in water, and whose solution tastes bitter, feels slippery, and can change the color of certain compounds.

Properties of Bases   If you have ever accidentally tasted soap, then you know the bitter taste of a base. Soap also demonstrates that a base feels slippery. However, NEVER use taste or touch as a test to identify an unknown chemical. Like acids, many bases are corrosive. If your fingers feel slippery when you are using a base in an experiment, you might have gotten the base on your hands. You should immediately rinse your hands with large amounts of water.

Solutions of bases conduct an electric current because bases increase the number of hydroxide ions, OH⁻, in a solution. A hydroxide ion is actually a hydrogen atom and an oxygen atom bonded together. An extra electron gives the ion a negative charge.

NEVER touch or taste a concentrated solution of a strong base.

Detecting Bases   Like acids, bases change the color of an indicator. Most indicators turn a different color for bases than they do for acids. For example, bases will change the color of red litmus paper to blue, as shown in **Figure 10.**

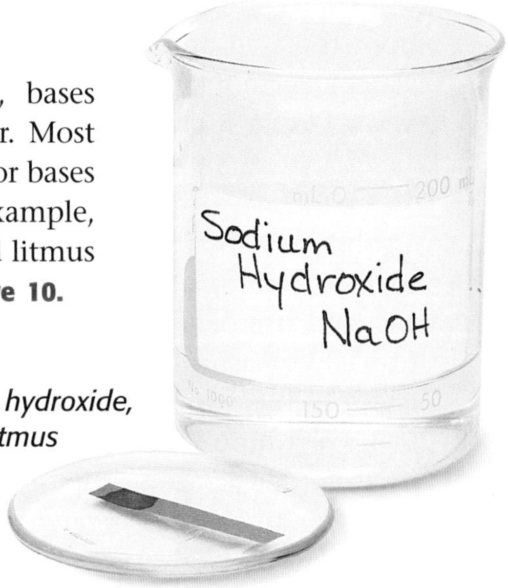

Figure 10 *Sodium hydroxide, a base, turns red litmus paper blue.*

Uses of Bases   Like acids, bases have many uses. Sodium hydroxide is used to make soap and paper. It is also in oven cleaners and in products that unclog drains, as shown in **Figure 11.** Remember, bases can harm your skin, so carefully follow the safety instructions when using these products. Calcium hydroxide is used to make cement, mortar, and plaster. Ammonia is found in many household cleaners and is also used in the production of fertilizers. Magnesium hydroxide and aluminum hydroxide are used in antacids to treat heartburn.

Figure 11 *This drain cleaner contains sodium hydroxide to help dissolve grease that can clog the drain.*

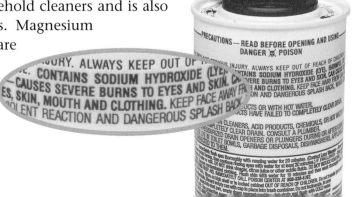

Strong Versus Weak When all the molecules of a base break apart in water to produce hydroxide ions, the base is called a strong base. Strong bases include sodium hydroxide, calcium hydroxide, and potassium hydroxide.

When only a few of the molecules of a base produce hydroxide ions in water, the base is called a weak base. Ammonia, magnesium hydroxide, and aluminum hydroxide are all weak bases.

Acids and Bases Neutralize One Another

If you have ever suffered from an acid stomach, or heartburn, as shown in **Figure 12,** you might have taken an antacid. Antacids contain weak bases that soothe your heartburn by reacting with and neutralizing the acid in your stomach. Acids and bases neutralize one another because the H^+ of the acid and the OH^- of the base react to form water, H_2O. Other ions from the acid and base are also dissolved in the water. If the water is evaporated, these ions join to form a compound called a salt. You'll learn more about salts later in this section.

The pH Scale Indicators such as litmus can identify whether a solution contains an acid or base. To describe how acidic or basic a solution is, the pH scale is used. The **pH** of a solution is a measure of the hydronium ion concentration in the solution. By measuring the hydronium ion concentration, the pH is also a measure of the hydrogen ion concentration. On the scale, a solution that has a pH of 7 is neutral, meaning that it is neither acidic nor basic. Pure water has a pH of 7. Basic solutions have a pH greater than 7, and acidic solutions have a pH less than 7. Look at **Figure 13** to see the pH values for many common materials.

Figure 12 *Have heartburn? Take an antacid! Antacid tablets contain a base that neutralizes the acid in your stomach.*

Figure 13 pH Values of Common Materials

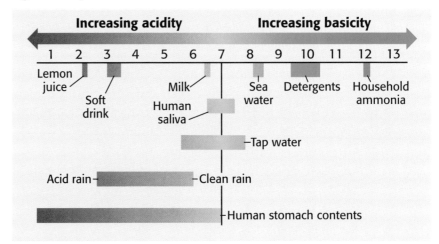

Using Indicators to Determine pH A single indicator allows you to determine if a solution is acidic or basic, but a mixture of different indicators can be used to determine the pH of a solution. After determining the colors for this mixture at different pH values, the indicators can be used to determine the pH of an unknown solution, as shown in **Figure 14.** Indicators can be used as paper strips or solutions, and they are often used to test the pH of soil and of water in pools and aquariums. Another way to determine the acidity of a solution is to use an instrument called a pH meter, which can detect and measure hydrogen ions electronically.

Figure 14 *The paper strip contains several indicators. The pH of a solution is determined by comparing the color of the strip to the scale provided.*

✔ Self-Check

Which is more acidic, a soft drink or milk? (Hint: Refer to Figure 13 to find the pH values of these drinks.) *(See page 136 to check your answer.)*

Biology CONNECTION

Human blood has a pH of between 7.38 and 7.42. If the pH is above 7.8 or below 7, the body cannot function properly. Sudden changes in blood pH that are not quickly corrected can be fatal.

pH and the Environment Living things depend on having a steady pH in their environment. Plants are known to have certain preferred growing conditions. Some plants, such as pine trees, prefer acidic soil with a pH between 4 and 6. Other plants, such as lettuce, require basic soil with a pH between 8 and 9. Fish require water near pH 7. As you can see in Figure 13, rainwater can have a pH as low as 3. This occurs in areas where compounds found in pollution react with water to make the strong acids sulfuric acid and nitric acid. As this acid precipitation collects in lakes, it can lower the pH to levels that may kill the fish and other organisms in the lake. To neutralize the acid and bring the pH closer to 7, a base can be added to the lakes, as shown in **Figure 15.**

Figure 15 *This helicopter is adding a base to an acidic lake. Neutralizing the acid in the lake might help protect the organisms living in the lake.*

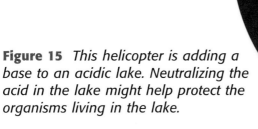

Chemical Compounds **61**

Salts

When you hear the word *salt,* you probably think of the table salt you use to season your food. But the sodium chloride found in your salt shaker is only one example of a large group of compounds called salts. A **salt** is an ionic compound formed from the positive ion of a base and the negative ion of an acid. You may remember that a salt and water are produced when an acid neutralizes a base. However, salts can also be produced in other reactions, as shown in **Figure 16.**

Figure 16 *The salt potassium chloride can be formed from several different reactions.*

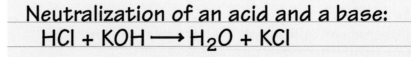

Neutralization of an acid and a base:
$$HCl + KOH \longrightarrow H_2O + KCl$$

Reaction of a metal with an acid:
$$2K + 2HCl \longrightarrow 2KCl + H_2$$

Reaction of a metal and a nonmetal:
$$2K + Cl_2 \longrightarrow 2KCl$$

Uses of Salts Salts have many uses in industry and in your home. You already know that sodium chloride is used to season foods. It is also used in the production of other compounds, including lye (sodium hydroxide), hydrochloric acid, and baking soda. The salt calcium sulfate is made into wallboard, or plasterboard, which is used in construction. Sodium nitrate is one of many salts used as a preservative in foods. Calcium carbonate is a salt that makes up limestone, chalk, and seashells. Another use of salts is shown in **Figure 17.**

Figure 17 *Salts are used to help keep roads free of ice.*

SECTION REVIEW

1. What ion is present in all acid solutions?

2. What are two ways scientists can measure pH?

3. What products are formed when an acid and base react?

4. **Comparing Concepts** Compare the properties of acids and bases.

5. **Applying Concepts** Would you expect the pH of a solution of soap to be 4 or 9?

Organic Compounds

Terms to Learn

organic compounds
biochemicals   proteins
carbohydrates   nucleic acids
lipids   hydrocarbons

What You'll Do

◆ Explain why so many organic compounds are possible.
◆ Describe the characteristics of carbohydrates, lipids, proteins, and nucleic acids and their functions in the body.
◆ Describe and identify saturated, unsaturated, and aromatic hydrocarbons.

Of all the known compounds, more than 90 percent are members of a group of compounds called organic compounds. **Organic compounds** are covalent compounds composed of carbon-based molecules. Sugar, starch, oil, protein, nucleic acid, and even cotton and plastic are organic compounds. How can there be so many different kinds of organic compounds? The huge variety of organic compounds is explained by examining the carbon atom.

Each Carbon Atom Forms Four Bonds

Carbon atoms form the backbone of organic compounds. Because each carbon atom has four valence electrons (electrons in the outermost energy level of an atom), each atom can make four bonds. Thus, a carbon atom can bond to one, two, or even three other carbon atoms and still have electrons remaining to bond to other atoms. Three types of carbon backbones on which many organic compounds are based are shown in the models in **Figure 18.**

Some organic compounds have hundreds or even thousands of carbon atoms making up their backbone! Although the elements hydrogen and oxygen, along with carbon, make up many of the organic compounds, sulfur, nitrogen, and phosphorus are also important—especially in forming the molecules that make up all living things.

Figure 18 *These models, called structural formulas, are used to show how atoms in a molecule are connected. Each line represents a pair of electrons shared in a covalent bond.*

Straight Chain All carbon atoms are connected one after another in a line.

Branched Chain The chain of carbon atoms continues in more than one direction where a carbon atom bonds to three or more other carbon atoms.

Ring The chain of carbon atoms forms a ring.

Biochemicals: The Compounds of Life

Organic compounds made by living things are called **biochemicals.** The molecules of most biochemicals are very large. Biochemicals can be divided into four categories: carbohydrates, lipids, proteins, and nucleic acids. Each type of biochemical has important functions in living organisms.

Carbohydrates Starch and cellulose are examples of carbohydrates. **Carbohydrates** are biochemicals that are composed of one or more simple sugars bonded together; they are used as a source of energy and for energy storage. There are two types of carbohydrates: simple carbohydrates and complex carbohydrates. A single sugar molecule, represented using a hexagon, or a few sugar molecules bonded together are examples of simple carbohydrates, as illustrated in **Figure 19.** Glucose is a simple carbohydrate produced by plants through photosynthesis.

Figure 19 *The sugar molecules in the left image are simple carbohydrates. The starch in the right image is a complex carbohydrate because it is composed of many sugar molecules bonded together.*

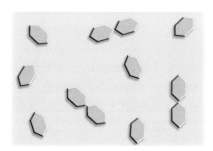 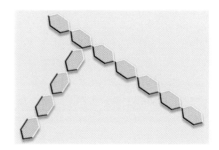

Sugar Storage System When an organism has more sugar than it needs, its extra sugar may be stored for later use in the form of complex carbohydrates, as shown in Figure 19. Molecules of complex carbohydrates are composed of hundreds or even thousands of sugar molecules bonded together. Because carbohydrates provide the energy you need each day, you should include sources of carbohydrates in your diet, such as the foods shown in **Figure 20.**

Figure 20 *Simple carbohydrates include sugars found in fruits and honey. Complex carbohydrates, such as starches, are found in bread, cereal, and pasta.*

Lipids Fats, oils, waxes, and steroids are examples of lipids. **Lipids** are biochemicals that do not dissolve in water and have many different functions, including storing energy and making up cell membranes. Although too much fat in your diet can be unhealthy, some fat is extremely important to good health. The foods in **Figure 21** are sources of lipids.

Lipids store excess energy in the body. Animals tend to store lipids primarily as fats, while plants store lipids as oils. When an organism has used up most of its carbohydrates, it can obtain energy by breaking down lipids. Lipids are also used to store vitamins that dissolve in fat but not in water.

Figure 21 *Vegetable oil, meat, cheese, nuts, and milk are sources of lipids in your diet.*

Lipids Make Up Cell Membranes Each cell is surrounded by a cell membrane. Much of the cell membrane is formed from molecules of phospholipids. The structure of these molecules plays an important part in the phospholipid's role in the cell membrane. The tail of a phospholipid molecule is a long, straight-chain carbon backbone composed only of carbon and hydrogen atoms. The tail is not attracted to water. The head of a phospholipid molecule is attracted to water because it is composed of phosphorus, oxygen, and nitrogen atoms in addition to carbon and hydrogen atoms. This results in the double layer of phospholipid molecules shown in the model in **Figure 22.** This arrangement of phospholipid molecules creates a barrier to help control the flow of chemicals into and out of the cell.

BRAIN FOOD

Deposits of the lipid cholesterol in the body have been linked to health problems such as heart disease. However, cholesterol is needed in nerve and brain tissue as well as to make certain hormones that regulate body processes such as growth.

Figure 22 *A cell membrane is composed primarily of two layers of phospholipid molecules.*

The **head** of each phospholipid molecule is attracted to water either inside or outside of the cell.

The **tail** of each phospholipid molecule is pushed against other tails because they are not attracted to water.

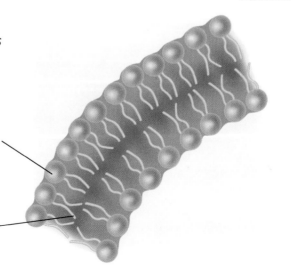

Figure 23 *Meat, fish, cheese, and beans contain proteins, which are broken down into amino acids as they are digested.*

Biology
C O N N E C T I O N

All the proteins in your body are made from just 20 amino acids. Nine of these amino acids are called essential amino acids because your body cannot make them. You must get them from the food you eat.

Proteins Most of the biochemicals found in living things are proteins. In fact, after water, proteins are the most abundant molecules in your cells. **Proteins** are biochemicals that are composed of amino acids; they have many different functions, including regulating chemical activities, transporting and storing materials, and providing structural support.

Every protein is composed of small "building blocks" called *amino acids*. Amino acids are smaller molecules composed of carbon, hydrogen, oxygen, and nitrogen atoms. Some amino acids also include sulfur atoms. Amino acids chemically bond to form proteins of many different shapes and sizes. The function of a protein depends on the shape that the bonded amino acids adopt. If even a single amino acid is missing or out of place, the protein may not function correctly or at all. The foods shown in **Figure 23** provide amino acids that your body needs to make new proteins.

Examples of Proteins Enzymes are proteins that regulate chemical reactions in the body by acting as catalysts to increase the rate at which the reactions occur. Some hormones are proteins. Insulin is a hormone that helps regulate the level of sugar in your blood. Oxygen is carried by the protein hemoglobin, allowing red blood cells to deliver oxygen throughout your body. There are also large proteins that extend through cell membranes and help control the transport of materials into and out of cells. Proteins that provide structural support often form structures that are easy to see, like those in **Figure 24**.

Figure 24 *Hair and spider webs are made up of proteins that are shaped like long fibers.*

Nucleic Acids The largest molecules made by living organisms are nucleic acids. **Nucleic acids** are biochemicals that store information and help to build proteins and other nucleic acids. Nucleic acids are sometimes called the "blueprints of life" because they contain all the information needed for the cell to make all of its proteins.

Like proteins, nucleic acids are long chains of smaller molecules joined together. These smaller molecules are composed of carbon, hydrogen, oxygen, nitrogen, and phosphorus atoms. Nucleic acids are much larger than proteins even though nucleic acids are composed of only five building blocks.

DNA and RNA There are two types of nucleic acids: DNA and RNA. DNA (**d**eoxyribo**n**ucleic **a**cid), like that shown in **Figure 25,** is the genetic material of the cell. DNA molecules can store an enormous amount of information because of their length. The DNA molecules in a single human cell have an overall length of about 2 m—that's over 6 ft long! When a cell needs to make a certain protein, it copies the important part of the DNA. The information copied from the DNA directs the order in which amino acids are bonded together to make that protein. DNA also contains information used to build the second type of nucleic acid, RNA (**r**ibo**n**ucleic **a**cid). RNA is involved in the actual building of proteins.

Science CONNECTION

Nucleic acids store information—even about ancient peoples. Read more about these incredible biochemicals on page 76.

Figure 25 *The DNA from a fruit fly contains all of the instructions for making proteins, nucleic acids . . . in fact, for making everything in the organism!*

SECTION REVIEW

1. What are organic compounds?

2. What are the four categories of biochemicals?

3. What are two functions of proteins?

4. What biochemicals are used to provide energy?

5. **Inferring Relationships** Sickle-cell anemia is a condition that results from a change of one amino acid in the protein hemoglobin. Why is this condition a genetic disorder?

Hydrocarbons

Organic compounds that are composed of only carbon and hydrogen are called **hydrocarbons.** Hydrocarbons are an important group of organic compounds. Many fuels, including gasoline, methane, and propane, are hydrocarbons. Hydrocarbons can be divided into three categories: saturated, unsaturated, and aromatic.

Saturated Hydrocarbons   Propane, like that used in the stove in **Figure 26,** is an example of a saturated hydrocarbon. A *saturated hydrocarbon* is a hydrocarbon in which each carbon atom in the molecule shares a single bond with each of four other atoms. A single bond is a covalent bond that consists of one pair of shared electrons. Hydrocarbons that contain carbon atoms connected only by single bonds are called saturated because no other atoms can be added without replacing an atom that is part of the molecule. Saturated hydrocarbons are also called *alkanes.*

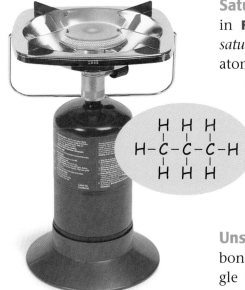

Figure 26 *The propane in this camping stove is a saturated hydrocarbon.*

Unsaturated Hydrocarbons   Each carbon atom forms four bonds. However, these bonds do not always have to be single bonds. An *unsaturated hydrocarbon* is a hydrocarbon in which at least two carbon atoms share a double bond or a triple bond. A double bond is a covalent bond that consists of two pairs of shared electrons. Compounds that contain two carbon atoms connected by a double bond are called *alkenes.*

A triple bond is a covalent bond that consists of three pairs of shared electrons. Hydrocarbons that contain two carbon atoms connected by a triple bond are called *alkynes.*

Hydrocarbons that contain double or triple bonds are called unsaturated because the double or triple bond can be broken to allow more atoms to be added to the molecule. Examples of unsaturated hydrocarbons are shown in **Figure 27.**

Figure 27 *Fruits produce ethene, which helps ripen the fruit. Ethyne, better known as acetylene, is burned in this miner's lamp and is also used in welding.*

Aromatic Hydrocarbons Most aromatic compounds are based on benzene, the compound represented by the model in **Figure 28.** Look for this structure to help identify an aromatic hydrocarbon. As the name implies, aromatic hydrocarbons often have strong odors and are therefore used in such products as air fresheners and moth balls.

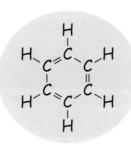

Figure 28 *Benzene has a ring of six carbons with alternating double and single bonds. Benzene is the starting material for manufacturing many products, including medicines.*

Other Organic Compounds

Many other types of organic compounds exist that have atoms of halogens, oxygen, sulfur, and phosphorus in their molecules. A few of these types of compounds and their uses are described in the chart below.

Types and Uses of Organic Compounds		
Type of compound	**Uses**	**Examples**
Alkyl halides	starting material for Teflon refrigerant (freon)	chloromethane (CH_3Cl) bromoethane (C_2H_5Br)
Alcohols	rubbing alcohol gasoline additive antifreeze	methanol (CH_3OH) ethanol (C_2H_5OH)
Organic acids	food preservatives flavorings	ethanoic acid (CH_3COOH) propanoic acid (C_2H_5COOH)
Esters	flavorings fragrances clothing (polyester)	methyl ethanoate (CH_3COOCH_3) ethyl propanoate ($C_2H_5COOC_2H_5$)

SECTION REVIEW

1. What is a hydrocarbon?

2. How many electrons are shared in a double bond? a triple bond?

3. **Comparing Concepts** Compare saturated and unsaturated hydrocarbons.

internet connect

SC*i*LINKS
NSTA

TOPIC: Organic Compounds
GO TO: www.scilinks.org
*sci*LINKS NUMBER: HSTP375

Skill Builder Lab

Cabbage Patch Indicators

Indicators are weak acids or bases that change color according to the pH of the substance to which they are added. Red cabbage contains a natural indicator. It turns specific colors at specific pHs. In this lab, you will extract the indicator from red cabbage. Then you will use it to find the pH of several liquids.

MATERIALS

- distilled water
- 250 mL beaker
- red cabbage leaf
- hot plate
- beaker tongs
- masking tape
- test tubes
- test-tube rack
- eyedropper
- sample liquids provided by teacher
- litmus paper

Procedure

1. Copy the table on the next page into your Science-Log, or construct a similar one using a computer. Include one line for each sample liquid you will test.

2. Put on protective gloves. Place 100 mL of distilled water in the beaker. Tear the cabbage leaf into small pieces. Place the pieces in the beaker.

3. Use the hot plate to bring the cabbage and water to a boil. Continue boiling until the water is deep blue.
   Caution: Use extreme care when working near a hot plate.

4. Use tongs to remove the beaker from the hot plate. Turn the hot plate off. Allow the solution to cool for 5–10 minutes.

5. While the solution is cooling, use masking tape and a pen to label the test tubes for each sample liquid. Label one test tube as the control. Place the tubes in the rack.

Data Collection Table			
Liquid	Color of indicator	pH	Effect on litmus paper
Control			

DO NOT WRITE IN BOOK

6 Use the eyedropper to place a small amount (about 5 mL) of the indicator (cabbage juice) in the test tube labeled as the control. Pour a small amount (about 5 mL) of each sample liquid into the appropriate test tube.

7 Using the eyedropper, place several drops of the indicator into each test tube. Swirl gently. Record in your table the color of each liquid. Use the chart below to find the pH for each sample. Record the pH levels.

8 Litmus paper has an indicator that turns red in an acid and blue in a base. Test each liquid with litmus paper. Record the results.

Analysis

9 What purpose does the control serve? What is the pH of the control?

10 What colors are associated with acids? with bases?

11 Why is red cabbage juice considered a good indicator?

12 Which do you think would be more useful to help identify an unknown liquid—litmus paper or red cabbage juice? Why?

Going Further

Unlike distilled water, rainwater has carbon dioxide dissolved in it. Is rainwater acidic, basic, or neutral? To find out, place a small amount of the cabbage juice indicator in a clean test tube. (The indicator is water-based.) Use a straw to gently blow bubbles in the indicator. Continue until you see a color change. What can you conclude about the pH of your "rainwater"? What is the purpose of blowing bubbles in the cabbage juice?

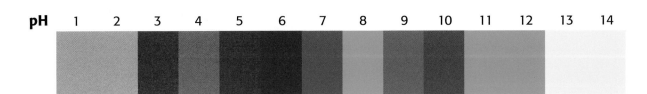

pH 1 2 3 4 5 6 7 8 9 10 11 12 13 14

Chapter Highlights

SECTION 1

Vocabulary
ionic compounds (*p. 54*)
covalent compounds (*p. 55*)

Section Notes

- Ionic compounds contain ionic bonds and are composed of oppositely charged ions arranged in a repeating pattern called a crystal lattice.

- Ionic compounds tend to be brittle, have high melting points, and dissolve in water to form solutions that conduct an electric current.

- Covalent compounds are composed of elements that are covalently bonded and consist of independent particles called molecules.

- Covalent compounds tend to have low melting points. Most do not dissolve well in water and do not form solutions that conduct an electric current.

SECTION 2

Vocabulary
acid (*p. 57*)
base (*p. 59*)
pH (*p. 60*)
salt (*p. 62*)

Section Notes

- An acid is a compound that increases the number of hydrogen ions in solution. Acids taste sour, turn blue litmus paper red, react with metals to produce hydrogen gas, and react with limestone or baking soda to produce carbon dioxide gas.

- A base is a compound that increases the number of hydroxide ions in solution. Bases taste bitter, feel slippery, and turn red litmus paper blue.

- When dissolved in water, every molecule of a strong acid or base breaks apart to form ions. Few molecules of weak acids and bases break apart to form ions.

- When combined, an acid and a base neutralize one another to produce water and a salt.

- pH is a measure of hydronium ion concentration in a solution. A pH of 7 indicates a neutral substance. A pH of less than 7 indicates an acidic substance. A pH of greater than 7 indicates a basic substance.

- A salt is an ionic compound formed from the positive ion of a base and the negative ion of an acid.

Labs
Making Salt (*p. 110*)

☑ Skills Check

Visual Understanding

LITMUS PAPER You can use the ability of acids and bases to change the color of indicators to identify a chemical as an acid or base. Litmus is an indicator commonly used in schools. Review Figures 8 and 10, which show how the color of litmus paper is changed by an acid and by a base.

pH SCALE Knowing whether a substance is an acid or a base can help explain some of the properties of the substance. The pH scale shown in Figure 13 illustrates the pH ranges for many common substances.

Vocabulary

organic compounds *(p. 63)*

biochemicals *(p. 64)*

carbohydrates *(p. 64)*

lipids *(p. 65)*

proteins *(p. 66)*

nucleic acids *(p. 67)*

hydrocarbons *(p. 68)*

Section Notes

- Organic compounds are covalent compounds composed of carbon-based molecules.

- Each carbon atom forms four bonds with other carbon atoms or with atoms of other elements to form straight chains, branched chains, or rings.

- Biochemicals are organic compounds made by living things.

- Carbohydrates are biochemicals that are composed of one or more simple sugars bonded together; they are used as a source of energy and for energy storage.

- Lipids are biochemicals that do not dissolve in water and have many functions, including storing energy and making up cell membranes.

- Proteins are biochemicals that are composed of amino acids and have many functions, including regulating chemical activities, transporting and storing materials, and providing structural support.

- Nucleic acids are biochemicals that store information and help to build proteins and other nucleic acids.

- Hydrocarbons are organic compounds composed of only carbon and hydrogen.

- In a saturated hydrocarbon, each carbon atom in the molecule shares a single bond with each of four other atoms.

- In an unsaturated hydrocarbon, at least two carbon atoms share a double bond or a triple bond.

- Many aromatic hydrocarbons are based on the six-carbon ring of benzene.

- Other organic compounds, including alkyl halides, alcohols, organic acids, and esters, are formed by adding atoms of other elements.

☑ internet connect

GO TO: go.hrw.com

Visit the **HRW** Web site for a variety of learning tools related to this chapter. Just type in the keyword:

KEYWORD: HSTCMP

GO TO: www.scilinks.org

Visit the **National Science Teachers Association** on-line Web site for Internet resources related to this chapter. Just type in the *sci*LINKS number for more information about the topic:

TOPIC: Ionic Compounds	*sci*LINKS NUMBER: HSTP355
TOPIC: Covalent Compounds	*sci*LINKS NUMBER: HSTP360
TOPIC: Acids and Bases	*sci*LINKS NUMBER: HSTP365
TOPIC: Salts	*sci*LINKS NUMBER: HSTP370
TOPIC: Organic Compounds	*sci*LINKS NUMBER: HSTP375

Chapter Review

To complete the following sentences, choose the correct term from each pair of terms listed below:

1. Compounds that have low melting points and do not usually dissolve well in water are ___?___. (*ionic compounds* or *covalent compounds*)

2. A(n) ___?___ turns red litmus paper blue. (*acid* or *base*)

3. ___?___ are composed of only carbon and hydrogen. (*Ionic compounds* or *Hydrocarbons*)

4. A biochemical composed of amino acids is a ___?___. (*lipid* or *protein*)

5. A source of energy for living things can be found in ___?___. (*nucleic acids* or *carbohydrates*)

UNDERSTANDING CONCEPTS

Multiple Choice

6. Which of the following describes lipids?
   a. used to store energy
   b. do not dissolve in water
   c. make up most of the cell membrane
   d. all of the above

7. An acid reacts to produce carbon dioxide when the acid is added to
   a. water.
   b. limestone.
   c. salt.
   d. sodium hydroxide.

8. Which of the following does NOT describe ionic compounds?
   a. high melting point
   b. brittle
   c. do not conduct electric currents in water
   d. dissolve easily in water

9. An increase in the concentration of hydronium ions in solution ___?___ the pH.
   a. raises
   b. lowers
   c. does not affect
   d. doubles

10. Which of the following compounds makes up the majority of cell membranes?
    a. lipids
    b. ionic compounds
    c. acids
    d. nucleic acids

11. The compounds that store information for building proteins are
    a. lipids.
    b. hydrocarbons.
    c. nucleic acids.
    d. carbohydrates.

Short Answer

12. What type of compound would you use to neutralize a solution of potassium hydroxide?

13. Explain why the reaction of an acid with a base is called *neutralization*.

14. What characteristic of carbon atoms helps to explain the wide variety of organic compounds?

15. Compare acids and bases based on the ion produced when each compound is dissolved in water.

Concept Mapping

16. Use the following terms to create a concept map: acid, base, salt, neutral, pH.

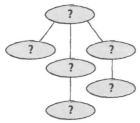

CRITICAL THINKING AND PROBLEM SOLVING

17. Fish give off the base ammonia, NH_3, as waste. How does the release of ammonia affect the pH of the water in the aquarium? What can be done to correct the problem?

18. Many insects, such as fire ants, inject formic acid, a weak acid, when they bite or sting. Describe the type of compound that should be used to treat the bite.

19. Organic compounds are also covalent compounds. What properties would you expect organic compounds to have as a result?

20. Farmers often can taste their soil to determine whether the soil has the correct acidity for their plants. How would taste help the farmer determine the acidity of the soil?

21. A diet that includes a high level of lipids is unhealthy. Why is a diet containing no lipids also unhealthy?

INTERPRETING GRAPHICS

Study the structural formulas below, and then answer the questions that follow.

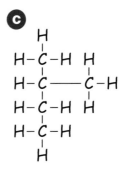

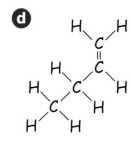

22. A saturated hydrocarbon is represented by which structural formula(s)?

23. An unsaturated hydrocarbon is represented by which structural formula(s)?

24. An aromatic hydrocarbon is represented by which structural formula(s)?

Reading Check-up

Take a minute to review your answers to the Pre-Reading Questions found at the bottom of page 52. Have your answers changed? If necessary, revise your answers based on what you have learned since you began this chapter.

Unique Compounds

What makes you unique? Would you believe it's a complex pattern of information found on the deoxyribonucleic acid (DNA) in your cells? Well it is! And by analyzing how this information is arranged, scientists are finding clues about human ancestry.

Mummy Knows Best

If you compare the DNA from an older species and a more recent species, you can tell which traits were passed on. To consider the question of human evolution, scientists must use DNA from older humans—like mummies. Molecular archeologists study DNA from mummies in order to understand human evolution at a molecular level. Since well-preserved DNA fragments from mummies are scarce, you might be wondering why some ancient DNA fragments have been preserved better than others.

Neutralizing Acids

The condition of preserved DNA fragments depends on how the mummy was preserved. The tannic acid—commonly found in peat bogs—that is responsible for preserving mummies destroys DNA. But if there are limestone rocks nearby, the calcium carbonate from these rocks neutralizes the tannic acid, thereby preserving the DNA.

Molecular Photocopying

When scientists find well-preserved DNA, they make copies of it by using a technique called polymerase chain reaction (PCR). PCR takes advantage of *polymerases* to generate copies of DNA fragments. Polymerases are found in all living things, and their job is to make strands of genetic material using existing strands as templates. That is why PCR is also called molecular photocopying. But researchers who use this technique risk contaminating the ancient DNA with their own DNA. If even one skin cell falls into the PCR mixture, the results are ruined.

Mysteries Solved?

PCR has been used to research ancient civilizations and peoples. For example, scientists found an 8,000-year-old human brain in Florida. This brain was preserved well enough for scientists to analyze the DNA and to conclude that today's Native Americans are not direct descendants of this group of people.

PCR has also been used to analyze the culture of ancient peoples. When archeologists tested the pigments used in 4,000-year-old paintings on rocks along the Pecos River, in Texas, they found DNA that was probably from bison. This was an unexpected discovery because there were no bison along the Pecos River when the paintings were made. The archeologists have concluded, therefore, that the artists must have tried very hard to find this specific pigment for their paint. This leads the archeologists to believe that the paintings must have had some spiritual meaning.

On Your Own

▶ Research ways PCR is being used to detect diseases and infections in humans and animals.

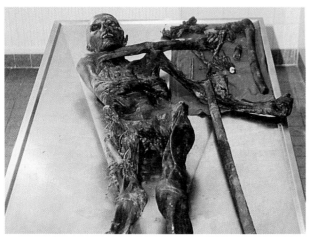

▲ *DNA from mummies like this one provides scientists with valuable information.*

THE SECRETS OF SPIDER SILK

What is as strong as steel, more elastic than a rubber band, and able to stop a speeding bullet? Spider silk! Spiders make this silk to weave their delicate but deadly webs.

▲ *A golden orb-weaving spider on its web*

The Tangled Web We Weave

If you've seen a spider web, you've probably noticed that it resembles a bicycle wheel. The "spokes" of the web are made of a silk thread called *dragline silk.* The sticky, stretchy part of the web is called *capture silk* because that's what spiders use to capture their prey. Spider silk is made of proteins, and these proteins are made of blocks of amino acids.

There are 20 naturally occurring amino acids, but spider silk has only seven of them. Until recently, scientists knew what the silk is made of, but they didn't know how these amino acids were distributed throughout the protein chains.

Scientists used a technique called nuclear magnetic resonance (NMR) to see the structure of dragline silk. The silk fiber is made of two tough strands of alanine-rich protein embedded in a glycine-rich substance. If you look at this protein even closer, it looks like tangled spaghetti. Scientists believe that this tangled part makes the silk springy and a repeating sequence of five amino acids makes the protein stretchy.

Spinning Tails

Scientists think they have identified the piece of DNA needed to make the spider silk. Synthetic silk can be made by copying a small part of this DNA and inserting it into the bacterium *Escherichia coli.* The bacteria read the gene and make liquid silk protein. Biologists at the University of Wyoming in Laramie have come up with a way to spin spider silk into threads by pushing the liquid protein through fine tubes.

What Do You Think?

▶ Scientists seem to think that there are many uses for synthetic spider silk. Make a list in your ScienceLog of as many things as you can think of that this material would be good for.

▲ *Spiders use organs called spinnerets to spin their webs. This image of spinnerets was taken with a scanning electron microscope.*

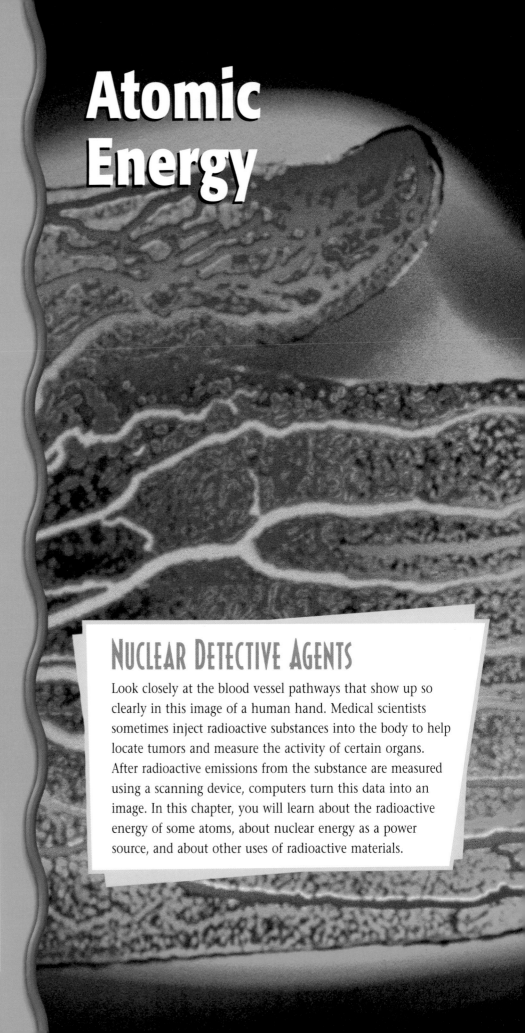

Atomic Energy

Pre-Reading Questions

1. What is nuclear radiation?
2. How are radioactive materials used?
3. What are two concerns about energy obtained from nuclear reactions?

NUCLEAR DETECTIVE AGENTS

Look closely at the blood vessel pathways that show up so clearly in this image of a human hand. Medical scientists sometimes inject radioactive substances into the body to help locate tumors and measure the activity of certain organs. After radioactive emissions from the substance are measured using a scanning device, computers turn this data into an image. In this chapter, you will learn about the radioactive energy of some atoms, about nuclear energy as a power source, and about other uses of radioactive materials.

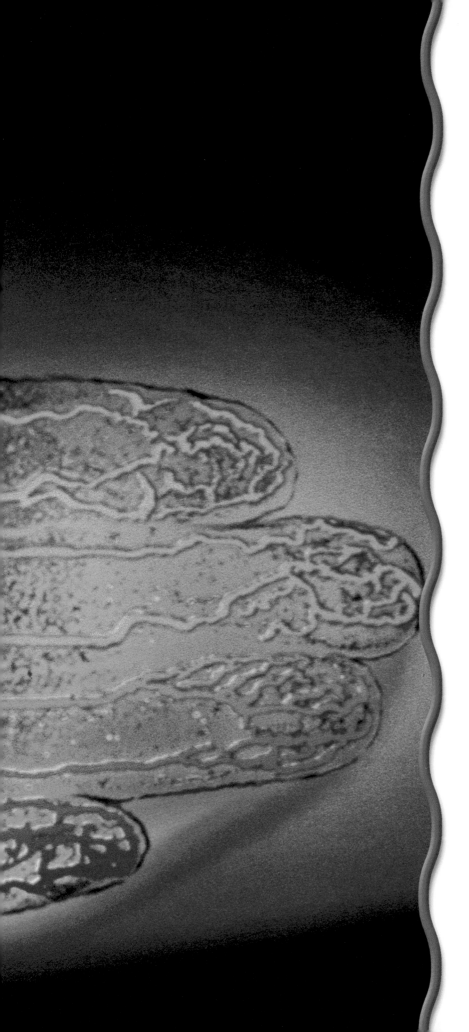

START-UP Activity

WATCH YOUR HEADSIUM!

The nuclei of radioactive atoms are unstable. Therefore, they decay and change into different nuclei. In this activity, you will model the decay of unstable nuclei into stable nuclei.

Procedure

1. Place **100 pennies** heads-up in a **box with a lid.** The pennies represent radioactive "headsium" nuclei. Record the 100 headsium nuclei present as Trial 0 in your ScienceLog.

2. Close the box, and shake it vigorously up and down for 5 seconds.

3. Open the box, and remove all of the "tailsium" nuclei, pennies that are tails-up. These pennies represent stable nuclei that result from decay. Count the number of headsium nuclei remaining, and record it in your ScienceLog as Trial 1.

4. Continue performing trials until you have no more pennies in the box or you have finished five trials, whichever comes first. Record all your results.

Analysis

5. On a piece of **graph paper,** graph your data by plotting "Number of headsium nuclei" on the *y*-axis and "Trial number" on the *x*-axis.

6. What trend do you see in the number of headsium nuclei over time?

7. Compare your graph with the graphs of other students in your class.

Atomic Energy   **79**

Terms to Learn

nuclear radiation   beta decay
radioactivity   isotopes
radioactive decay   gamma decay
alpha decay   half-life
mass number

What You'll Do

◆ Compare alpha, beta, and gamma decay.
◆ Describe the penetrating power of the three types of nuclear radiation.
◆ Calculate ages of objects using half-life.
◆ Identify uses of radioactive materials.

Radioactivity

When scientists perform experiments, they don't always get the results they expect. In 1896, a French scientist named Henri Becquerel did not get the results he expected, but he did discover a fascinating new area of science.

Discovering Radioactivity

Becquerel's hypothesis was that fluorescent minerals could give off X rays. (*Fluorescent* materials glow when exposed to light, as shown in **Figure 1.**) To test his hypothesis, Becquerel placed a fluorescent mineral on top of a photographic plate wrapped in paper. He placed the setup in bright sunlight.

Becquerel predicted that an image of the mineral would appear on the plate. After developing the plate, he saw the image he expected.

Figure 1 *The brightly colored portions of this sample are fluorescent in ultraviolet light.*

An Unexpected Result Becquerel tried to confirm his results, but cloudy weather delayed his plans. He placed his materials in a drawer. After several days, he developed the plate anyway. He was amazed to see a strong image, shown in **Figure 2.**

Becquerel's results showed that even without light, the mineral gave off energy that passed through paper and made an image on the plate. After more tests, Becquerel concluded that this energy comes from uranium, an element in the mineral.

Naming the Unexpected Scientists call this energy **nuclear radiation,** high-energy particles and rays that are emitted by the nuclei of some atoms. Marie Curie, a scientist working with Becquerel, named the ability of some elements to give off nuclear radiation **radioactivity.**

Figure 2 *The blurry image on this photographic plate surprised Becquerel.*

Nuclear Radiation Is Produced Through Decay

Radioactive decay is the process in which the nucleus of a radioactive atom releases nuclear radiation. Three types of radioactive decay are alpha decay, beta decay, and gamma decay.

Alpha Decay The release of an alpha particle from a nucleus is called **alpha decay.** An *alpha particle* consists of two protons and two neutrons, so it has a mass number of 4 and a charge of 2+. An alpha particle is identical to the nucleus of a helium atom. Many large radioactive nuclei give off alpha particles to become nuclei of atoms of different elements. One example is radium-226. (Remember that the number that follows the name of an element indicates the **mass number**—the sum of the protons and neutrons in an atom.)

Conservation in Decay Look at the model of alpha decay in **Figure 3.** This model illustrates two important features of all types of radioactive decay. First, the mass number is conserved. The sum of the mass numbers of the starting materials is always equal to the sum of the mass numbers of the products. Second, charge is conserved. The sum of the charges of the starting materials is always equal to the sum of the charges of the products.

C O N N E C T I O N

Alpha particles emitted during alpha decay eventually gain two electrons from nearby atoms and become helium atoms. Almost all of the helium in Earth's atmosphere formed from alpha particles emitted by nuclei of radioactive atoms.

Figure 3 Alpha Decay of Radium-226

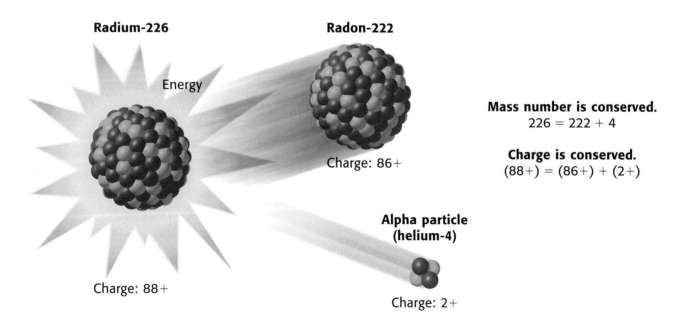

Radium-226

Radon-222

Energy

Charge: 86+

Charge: 88+

Alpha particle (helium-4)

Charge: 2+

Mass number is conserved.
226 = 222 + 4

Charge is conserved.
(88+) = (86+) + (2+)

Beta Decay   The release of a beta particle from a nucleus is called **beta decay.** A *beta particle* can be either an electron (having a charge of 1− and a mass of almost 0) or a *positron* (having a charge of 1+ and a mass of almost 0). Because electrons and positrons do not contain protons or neutrons, the mass number of a beta particle is 0.

Two Types of Beta Decay   A carbon-14 nucleus undergoes beta decay as shown in the model in **Figure 4.** During this decay, a neutron breaks into a proton and an electron. Notice that the nucleus becomes a nucleus of a different element, and mass number and charge are conserved, similar to alpha decay.

Not all isotopes of an element decay in the same way. (Remember that **isotopes** are atoms that have the same number of protons but different numbers of neutrons.) A carbon-11 nucleus undergoes beta decay when a proton breaks into a positron and a neutron. However, the beta decay of carbon-11 still changes the nucleus into a nucleus of a different element while conserving both mass number and charge.

Figure 4 Beta Decay of Carbon-14

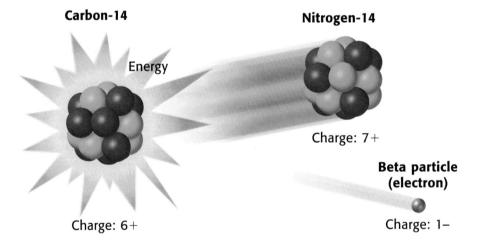

Mass number is conserved.
14 = 14 + 0

Charge is conserved.
(6+) = (7+) + (1−)

Carbon-14 — Energy — Nitrogen-14

Charge: 6+   Charge: 7+

Beta particle (electron)
Charge: 1−

Gamma Decay   Did you notice in Figures 3 and 4 that energy is released during alpha decay and beta decay? Some of this energy is in the form of *gamma rays,* a form of light with very high energy. The release of gamma rays from a nucleus is called **gamma decay.** Gamma decay occurs after alpha or beta decay as the particles in the nucleus shift to a more stable arrangement. Because gamma rays have no mass or charge, gamma decay alone does not cause one element to change into another as do alpha decay and beta decay.

✓ Self-Check

Which type of nuclear radiation has the largest mass number?
(See page 136 to check your answer.)

The Penetrating Power of Radiation

The three forms of nuclear radiation differ in their ability to penetrate (go through) matter. This difference is due to the mass and charge associated with each type of radiation, as you can see in **Figure 5.**

Figure 5 The Penetrating Abilities of Nuclear Radiation

Alpha particles have the greatest charge and mass. They travel about 7 cm through air and are stopped by paper or clothing.

Beta particles have a 1– or 1+ charge and almost no mass. They are more penetrating than alpha particles. They travel about 1 m through air, but are stopped by 3 mm of aluminum.

Gamma rays have no charge or mass and are the most penetrating. They are blocked by very dense, thick materials, such as a few centimeters of lead or a few meters of concrete.

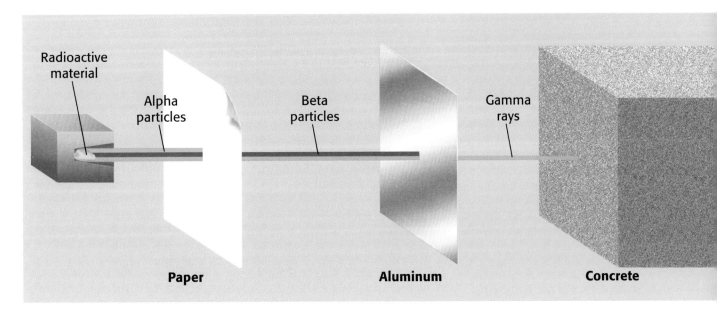

Radioactive material

Alpha particles

Beta particles

Gamma rays

Paper

Aluminum

Concrete

Effects of Radiation on Matter Nuclear radiation can "knock" electrons out of atoms and break chemical bonds between atoms. Both of these actions can cause damage to living and nonliving matter.

Damage to Living Matter When an organism absorbs radiation, its cells can be damaged, causing burns similar to those caused by touching a hot object. A single large exposure to radiation can lead to *radiation sickness*. Symptoms of this condition range from fatigue and loss of appetite to hair loss, destruction of blood cells, and even death. Exposure to radiation can also increase the risk of cancer because of the damage done to cells.

Marie and Irene Curie died of leukemia, a type of cancer in which abnormal white blood cells multiply and interfere with the body's immune system. It is thought that exposure to radiation caused their leukemia.

Environment
CONNECTION

Radioactive radon-222 forms from the radioactive decay of uranium found in soil and rocks. Because radon is a gas, it can enter buildings through gaps in the walls and floors. If radon is inhaled, the alpha particles emitted through alpha decay can damage sensitive lung tissue. In addition, solid polonium forms as radon decays. The polonium stays in the lungs and emits more alpha particles, greatly increasing the risk of cancer. Radon detectors are available to monitor radon levels in the home.

Damage to Nonliving Matter Radiation can also damage nonliving matter. When radiation knocks electrons out of metal atoms, the metal is weakened. The metal structures of buildings, such as nuclear power plants, can become unsafe. High levels of radiation, such as gamma rays from the sun, can damage space vehicles.

Damage at Different Depths Because gamma rays are the most penetrating nuclear radiation, they can cause damage deep within an object. Beta particles cause damage closer to the surface, while alpha particles cause damage very near the surface. However, if a source of alpha particles enters an organism, alpha particles cause the most damage because they are the largest and most massive radiation.

SECTION REVIEW

1. What is radioactivity?

2. What is meant by the phrase "mass number is conserved"?

3. **Comparing Concepts** Compare the penetrating power of the three types of nuclear radiation discussed.

Nuclei Decay to Become Stable

You already know that a nucleus consists of protons and neutrons together in a very small space. Protons have a positive charge, so they repel one another. (Remember, opposite charges attract, but like charges repel.) Why don't the protons fly apart? Because of the *strong force*, an attractive force that holds the protons and neutrons together in the nucleus.

Polonium
atomic number 84

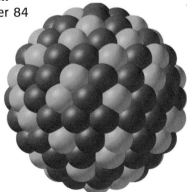

Too Many Protons The strong force acts only at extremely short distances. As a result, a large nucleus, as modeled in **Figure 6**, is often radioactive. In fact, all nuclei composed of more than 83 protons are radioactive. There are simply too many protons. Although some of these nuclei can exist for billions of years before they decay, they do eventually decay and are therefore called *unstable*.

Figure 6 *This nucleus is unstable, or radioactive, because the repulsion between the protons overcomes the strong force.*

Ratio of Neutrons to Protons A nucleus can also be unstable if it contains too many or too few neutrons compared with protons. Nuclei with more than 60 protons are stable when the ratio of neutrons to protons is about 3 to 2. Nuclei with fewer than 20 protons only need a ratio of about 1 to 1 for stability. This explains the existence of small radioactive isotopes, like the ones modeled in **Figure 7.**

How Does a Nucleus Become Stable? An unstable nucleus will emit (give off) nuclear radiation until it has a stable number of neutrons and protons. An unstable nucleus doesn't always achieve stability through one decay. In fact, some nuclei are just the first in a series of radioactive isotopes formed as a result of alpha and beta decays. Eventually, a nonradioactive nucleus is formed. The nuclei of the most common isotope of uranium, uranium-238, forms the nonradioactive nuclei of lead-206 after a series of 14 decays.

Hydrogen-3

2 neutrons
1 proton

Beryllium-10

6 neutrons
4 protons

Figure 7 *The ratio of neutrons to protons in hydrogen-3 and beryllium-10 is greater than 1 to 1. Therefore, the nuclei of these isotopes are unstable.*

Finding a Date by Decay

Finding a date for someone can be challenging—especially if they are several thousand years old! When hikers in the Italian Alps found the remains shown in **Figure 8** in 1991, scientists were able to estimate the time of death—about 5,300 years ago! How did they do this? The decay of radioactive carbon was the key.

Figure 8 *The remains of the Iceman, a 5,300-year-old mummy, are the best preserved of a human from that time.*

Carbon-14—It's in You! Carbon atoms are found in all living things. A small percentage of these atoms are radioactive carbon-14 atoms. During an organism's life, the percentage of carbon-14 in the organism stays about the same because the atoms that decay are replaced by atoms taken in from the atmosphere by plants or from food by animals. But when an organism dies, the carbon-14 is no longer replaced. Over time, the level of carbon-14 in the remains drops through decay.

Decay Occurs at a Steady Rate Scientists have determined that every 5,730 years, half of the carbon-14 in a sample decays. The rate of decay is constant and is not affected by other conditions, such as temperature or pressure. Each radioactive isotope has its own rate of decay, called half-life. A **half-life** is the amount of time it takes for one-half of the nuclei of a radioactive isotope to decay. **Figure 9** is a model of this process. The table below lists some radioactive isotopes with a wide range of half-lives.

Figure 9 *Half of any radioactive sample decays during each half-life.*

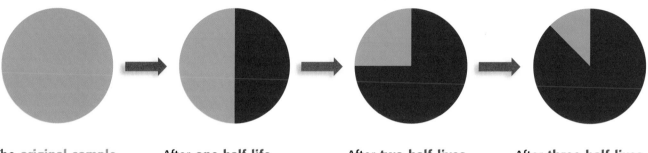

The original sample contains a certain amount of radioactive isotope.

After **one half-life,** one-half of the original sample has decayed, leaving half unchanged.

After **two half-lives,** one-fourth of the original sample remains unchanged.

After **three half-lives,** only one-eighth of the original sample remains unchanged.

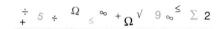

MATH BREAK

How Old Is It?

An antler has one-fourth of its original carbon-14 unchanged. As shown in Figure 9, two half-lives have occurred. To determine the age of the antler, multiply the number of half-lives that have passed by the length of a half-life. The antler's age is two times the half-life of carbon-14:

2 × 5,730 years = 11,460 years

Now It's Your Turn

Determine the age of a spear containing one-eighth its original amount of carbon-14.

Examples of Half-lives			
Isotope	**Half-life**	**Isotope**	**Half-life**
Uranium-238	4.5 billion years	Polonium-210	138 days
Oxygen-21	3.14 seconds	Nitrogen-13	10 minutes
Hydrogen-3	12.3 years	Calcium-36	0.1 second

Determining Age By measuring the number of decays each minute, scientists determined that a little less than half of the carbon-14 in the Iceman's body had decayed. This means that not quite one complete half-life (5,730 years) had passed since he died. You can try your hand at determining ages with the MathBreak at left.

Carbon-14 can be used to determine the age of objects up to 50,000 years old. To calculate the age of older objects, other elements must be used. For example, potassium-40, with a half-life of 1.3 billion years, is used to date dinosaur fossils.

Radioactivity and Your World

Although radioactivity can be dangerous, it also has positive uses. Most medical and industrial uses involve small amounts of nuclei with very short half-lives, so human exposure is low. Keep in mind that there are risks involved, but often, the benefits outweigh the risks.

Uses of Radioactivity You have learned how radioactive isotopes are used to determine the age of objects. Some isotopes can be used as *tracers*— radioactive elements whose paths can be followed through a process or reaction. Tracers help farmers determine how well plants take in elements from fertilizers. Tracers also help doctors diagnose medical problems, as shown in **Figure 10.** Radiation detectors are needed to locate the radioactive material in the organism.

Radioactive isotopes can also help detect defects in structures. For example, radiation is used to test the thickness of metal sheets as they are made. Another structure-testing use of radioactive isotopes is shown in **Figure 11.** More uses of radioactive isotopes are listed in the chart below.

Figure 10
This scan of a thyroid was made using radioactive iodine-131. The dark area shows the location of a tumor.

Figure 11 *Engineers can find weak spots in materials and leaks in pipes by detecting a tracer using a Geiger counter.*

More Uses of Radioactive Isotopes	
■ Killing cancer cells	■ Detecting smoke
■ Sterilizing food and health-care products	■ Powering space probes

SECTION REVIEW

1. What is a half-life?

2. Give two examples each of how radioactivity is useful and how it is harmful.

3. How many half-lives have passed if a sample contains one-eighth of its original amount of radioactive material?

4. **Doing Calculations** A rock contains one-fourth of its original amount of potassium-40. Calculate the rock's age if the half-life of potassium-40 is 1.3 billion years.

internet connect

SCiLINKS
NSTA

TOPIC: Discovering Radioactivity, Radioactive Isotopes
GO TO: www.scilinks.org
*sci*LINKS NUMBER: HSTP380, HSTP385

Terms to Learn

nuclear fission
nuclear chain reaction
nuclear fusion

What You'll Do

◆ Describe the process of nuclear fission.

◆ Describe the process of nuclear fusion.

◆ Identify advantages and disadvantages of energy from the nucleus.

Energy from the Nucleus

From an early age, you were probably told not to play with fire. But fire itself is neither good nor bad, it simply has benefits and hazards. Likewise, getting energy from the nucleus has benefits and hazards. In this section you will learn about two methods used to get energy from the nucleus—fission and fusion. Gaining an understanding of their advantages and disadvantages is important for people who will make decisions regarding the use of this energy—people like you!

Nuclear Fission

Not all unstable nuclei decay by releasing an alpha or beta particle or gamma rays. The nuclei of some atoms decay by breaking into two smaller, more stable nuclei during a process called nuclear fission. **Nuclear fission** is the process in which a large nucleus splits into two smaller nuclei with the release of energy.

The nuclei of uranium atoms, as well as the nuclei of other large atoms, can undergo nuclear fission naturally. They can also be made to undergo fission by hitting them with neutrons, as shown by the model in **Figure 12.**

Figure 12 Fission of a Uranium-235 Nucleus

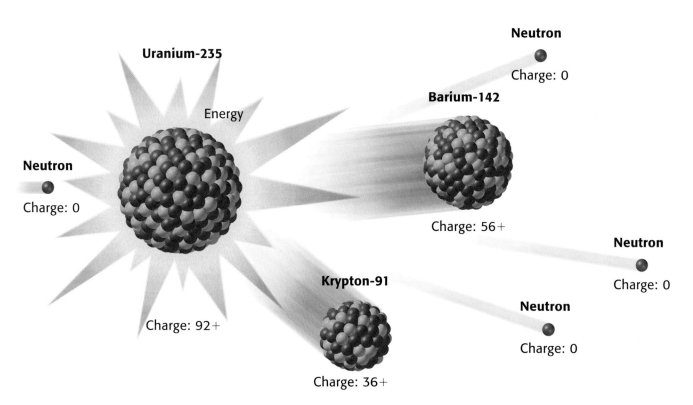

Uranium-235

Energy

Neutron
Charge: 0

Charge: 92+

Neutron
Charge: 0

Barium-142
Charge: 56+

Krypton-91
Charge: 36+

Neutron
Charge: 0

Neutron
Charge: 0

Energy from Matter Did you know that matter can be changed into energy? It's true! If you could determine the total mass of the products in Figure 12 and compare it with the total mass of the reactants, you would find something strange. The products have a tiny bit less mass than the reactants. Why are the masses different? Some of the matter was converted into energy.

The amount of energy released when a single uranium nucleus splits is not very great. But, keep in mind that this energy comes from an incredibly tiny amount of matter—about one-fifth of the mass of a hydrogen atom, the smallest atom that exists. In **Figure 13** you'll see an example of how small amounts of matter can yield large amounts of energy through nuclear fission.

Nuclear Chain Reactions Look at Figure 12 again. Suppose that two or three of the neutrons produced split other uranium-235 nuclei, which released energy and some neutrons. And then suppose that two or three of *those* neutrons split other nuclei, and so on. This situation is one type of **nuclear chain reaction**—a continuous series of nuclear fission reactions. A model of an uncontrolled chain reaction is shown in **Figure 14.**

Figure 13 *The nuclear fission of the uranium nuclei in one fuel pellet releases as much energy as the chemical change of burning about 1,000 kg of coal!*

Figure 14 *A chain reaction results in the release of an enormous amount of energy.*

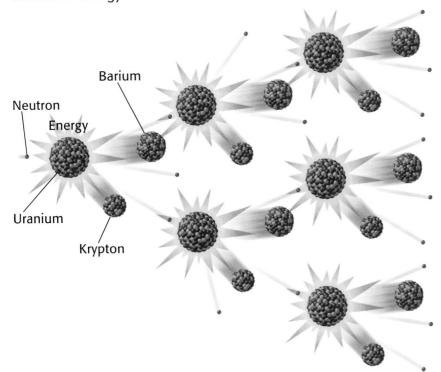

Barium

Neutron
Energy

Uranium

Krypton

Quick Lab

Gone Fission

1. Make two paper balls from a **sheet of paper.**

2. Stand in a group, arm's length apart, with your classmates.

3. Your teacher will gently toss one paper ball into the group. If you are touched by a ball, gently toss your paper balls into the group.

4. Explain how this activity is a model of a chain reaction. Be sure to explain what the students and the paper balls represent.

Energy from a Chain Reaction In an uncontrolled chain reaction, huge amounts of energy are released very quickly. In fact, the tremendous energy of an atomic bomb is the result of an uncontrolled chain reaction. In contrast, nuclear power plants use controlled chain reactions. The energy released from the nuclei in the uranium fuel is used to generate electrical energy. **Figure 15** shows how a nuclear power plant works.

Nuclear Versus Fossil Fuel Although nuclear power plants are more expensive to build than power plants using fossil fuels, they are often less expensive to operate because less fuel is needed. Also, nuclear power plants do not release gases, such as carbon dioxide, into the atmosphere. The use of fission extends our supply of fossil fuels. However, the supply of uranium is limited. Many nations rely on nuclear power to supply their energy needs. Nuclear power plants provide about 20 percent of the electrical energy used in the United States.

Figure 15 How a Nuclear Power Plant Works

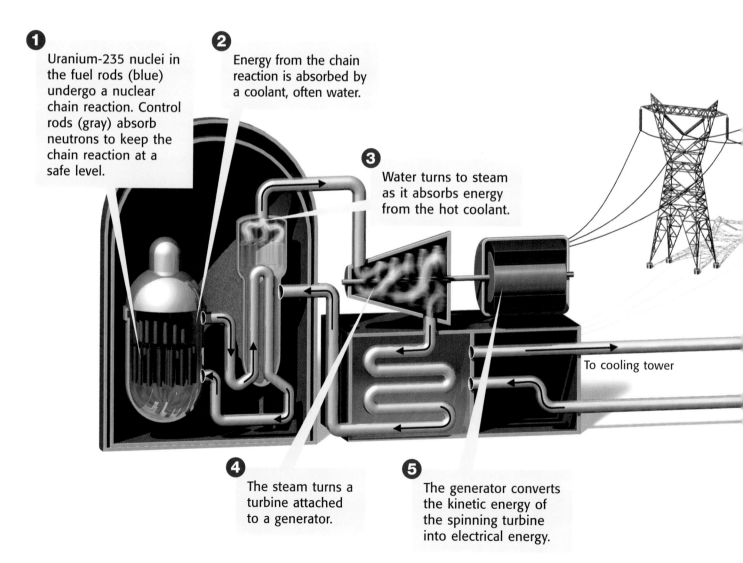

❶ Uranium-235 nuclei in the fuel rods (blue) undergo a nuclear chain reaction. Control rods (gray) absorb neutrons to keep the chain reaction at a safe level.

❷ Energy from the chain reaction is absorbed by a coolant, often water.

❸ Water turns to steam as it absorbs energy from the hot coolant.

To cooling tower

❹ The steam turns a turbine attached to a generator.

❺ The generator converts the kinetic energy of the spinning turbine into electrical energy.

Accidents Can Happen With the advantages described, why is fission not more widely used? Well, there are risks involved with generating electrical energy from fission. Probably the most immediate concern is the possibility of an accident. This fear was realized in Chernobyl, Ukraine, on April 26, 1986, as shown in **Figure 16.** An explosion released large amounts of radioactive uranium fuel and waste products into the atmosphere. The cloud of radioactive material spread over most of Europe and Asia and even reached as far as North America.

Figure 16 *During a test at the Chernobyl nuclear power plant, the emergency protection system was turned off. The reactor overheated, resulting in an explosion.*

What Waste! Another concern is nuclear waste, including used fuel rods, chemicals used to process uranium, and even shoe covers and overalls worn by workers. Although artificial fission has been carried out for only about 50 years, the waste will give off high levels of radiation for thousands of years. The rate of radioactive decay cannot be changed, so the waste must be stored until it becomes less radioactive. Most of the used fuel rods are stored in huge vats of water. Some of the liquid wastes are stored in underground tanks. However, scientists continue to look for more long-term storage solutions.

What would you say if a nuclear waste storage facility was planned near your town? Read about the debate over Yucca Mountain on page 100.

Storage Site Selection

A law that passed in 1987 requires the United States government to build a large underground storage facility to store nuclear waste. Imagine that you are a scientist in charge of finding a location for the site. Describe the characteristics of a good location. Keep in mind that the waste will need to be stored for a very long time without escaping into the environment.

Nuclear Fusion

Fusion is another nuclear reaction in which matter is converted into energy. In the process of **nuclear fusion,** two or more nuclei with small masses join together, or *fuse,* to form a larger, more massive nucleus.

In order for fusion to occur, the repulsion between positively charged nuclei must be overcome. That requires unbelievably high temperatures—over 100,000,000°C! But you already know a place where such temperatures are reached— the sun. In the sun's core, hydrogen nuclei fuse to form a helium nucleus, as shown in the model in **Figure 17.**

Astronomy

C O N N E C T I O N

Hydrogen is not the only fuel stars use for fusion. As a star gets older, its supply of hydrogen runs low and it begins to fuse larger atoms, such as helium, carbon, and silicon.

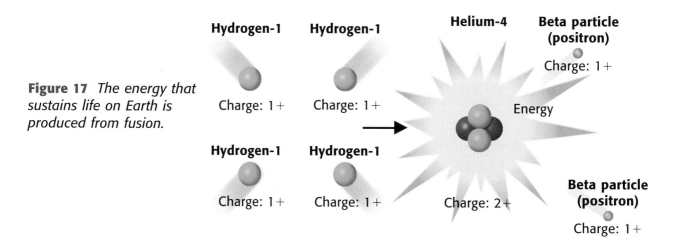

Figure 17 *The energy that sustains life on Earth is produced from fusion.*

Hydrogen-1 Charge: 1+
Hydrogen-1 Charge: 1+
Hydrogen-1 Charge: 1+
Hydrogen-1 Charge: 1+

Helium-4 Charge: 2+
Energy
Beta particle (positron) Charge: 1+
Beta particle (positron) Charge: 1+

Energy from Fusion? Energy for your home cannot yet be generated using nuclear fusion. First, incredibly high temperatures are needed. At these temperatures, hydrogen is a plasma, the state of matter in which electrons have been removed from atoms. No material on Earth can hold this plasma—imagine trying to bottle up plasma from the sun! **Figure 18** shows equipment used by researchers to try to contain plasma. Second, more energy is needed to create and contain the plasma than is produced by fusion. In spite of these problems, scientists predict that fusion will be used to provide electrical energy—possibly in your lifetime!

Figure 18 *Electric current in large coils of wire produces a strong magnetic field that can contain plasma.*

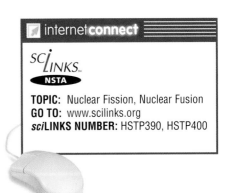

Oceans of Fuel Unlike nuclear fission, there is little concern about running out of fuel for nuclear fusion. Although the hydrogen-2 and hydrogen-3 isotopes used as fuel are much less common than hydrogen-1, there is still enough hydrogen in the waters of oceans and lakes to provide fuel for millions of years. In addition, a fusion reaction releases more energy than a fission reaction per gram of fuel, allowing for even greater savings of other resources, as shown in **Figure 19.**

Figure 19 *The energy generated by the fusion of the hydrogen-2 in 3.8 L (1 gal) of water would be about the same amount of energy generated by the chemical change of burning 1,140 L (300 gal) of gasoline!*

Less Accident Prone The concern over an accident such as the one at Chernobyl is much lower for fusion reactors. If an explosion occurred, there would be very little release of radioactive materials. The radioactive hydrogen-3 used for fuel in experimental fusion reactors is much less radioactive than the uranium fuel used in fission reactors.

Less Waste In addition to the advantages mentioned above, the products of fusion reactions are not radioactive, so there would be much less radioactive waste to worry about. This would make fusion an even "cleaner" source of energy than fission. While fusion has many benefits over fission as an energy source, large amounts of money will be required to pay for the research to make fusion possible.

SECTION REVIEW

1. Which nuclear reaction is currently used to generate electrical energy?

2. Which nuclear reaction is the source of the sun's energy?

3. What particle is needed to begin a nuclear chain reaction?

4. In both fission and fusion, what is converted into energy?

5. **Comparing Concepts** Compare the processes of nuclear fission and nuclear fusion.

internet**connect**

SC*I*LINKS.
NSTA

TOPIC: Nuclear Fission, Nuclear Fusion
GO TO: www.scilinks.org
*sci*LINKS NUMBER: HSTP390, HSTP400

Domino Chain Reactions

Fission of uranium-235 is a process that relies on neutrons. When a uranium-235 nucleus splits into two smaller nuclei, it releases two or three neutrons that can cause neighboring nuclei to undergo fission. This can result in a nuclear chain reaction. In this lab, you will use dominoes to build two models of nuclear chain reactions.

MATERIALS

- 15 dominoes
- stopwatch

Conduct an Experiment

1 For the first model, set up the dominoes as shown below. Each domino should hit two dominoes in the next row when pushed over.

2 Measure the time it takes for all of the dominoes to fall. To do this, start the stopwatch as you tip over the front domino. Stop the stopwatch when the last domino falls. Record this time in your ScienceLog.

3 If some of the dominoes do not fall, repeat steps 1 and 2. You may have to adjust the setup a few times.

4 For the second model, set up the dominoes as shown at left. The domino in the first row should hit both of the dominoes in the second row. Beginning with the second row, only one domino from each row should hit both of the dominoes in the next row.

5 Repeat step 2. Again, you may have to adjust the setup a few times to get all the dominoes to fall.

Analyze Your Results

6 Which model represents an uncontrolled chain reaction? Which represents a controlled chain reaction? Explain your answers.

7 Imagine that each domino releases a certain amount of energy as it falls. Compare the total amount of energy released in the two models.

8 Compare the time needed to release the energy in the models. Which model had the longest time? Which model had the shortest time?

Draw Conclusions

9 In a nuclear power plant, a chain reaction is controlled by using a material that absorbs neutrons. Only enough neutrons to continue the chain reaction are allowed to produce further fission of uranium-235. Explain how your model of a controlled nuclear chain reaction modeled this process.

10 Why must uranium nuclei be close to each other in order for a nuclear chain reaction to occur? (Hint: What would happen in your model if the dominoes were too far apart?)

Chapter Highlights

Vocabulary

nuclear radiation *(p. 80)*

radioactivity *(p. 80)*

radioactive decay *(p. 81)*

alpha decay *(p. 81)*

mass number *(p. 81)*

beta decay *(p. 82)*

isotopes *(p. 82)*

gamma decay *(p. 82)*

half-life *(p. 86)*

Section Notes

- Radioactive nuclei give off nuclear radiation in the form of alpha particles, beta particles, and gamma rays through a process called radioactive decay.

- During alpha decay, an alpha particle is released from the nucleus. An alpha particle is composed of two protons and two neutrons.

- During beta decay, a beta particle is released from the nucleus. A beta particle can be an electron or a positron.

- Gamma decay occurs with alpha decay and beta decay when particles in the nucleus rearrange and emit energy in the form of gamma rays.

- Gamma rays penetrate matter better than alpha or beta particles. Beta particles penetrate matter better than alpha particles.

- Nuclear radiation can damage living and nonliving matter.

- Half-life is the amount of time it takes for one-half of the nuclei of a radioactive isotope to decay. The age of some objects can be determined using half-lives.

- Uses of radioactive materials include detecting defects in materials, sterilizing products, tracing a plant's or animal's use of an element, diagnosing illness, and producing electrical energy.

☑ Skills Check

Math Concepts

HALF-LIFE Radioactive decay occurs at a steady rate. To calculate the time that has passed, multiply the number of half-lives by the length of a half-life. For example, a radioactive isotope has a half-life of 10 days. If one-eighth of the original sample remains, then three half-lives have passed. The time that has passed is:

$$3 \times 10 \text{ days} = 30 \text{ days}$$

Visual Understanding

FISSION VERSUS FUSION The changes that occur in nuclear fission and nuclear fusion are very different. Review Figure 12 on page 88 and Figure 17 on page 92 to better understand the starting materials, products, and process involved in fission and fusion.

Vocabulary

nuclear fission *(p. 88)*

nuclear chain reaction *(p. 89)*

nuclear fusion *(p. 92)*

Section Notes

- Nuclear fission occurs when a massive, unstable nucleus breaks into two less massive nuclei. Nuclear fission is used in power plants to generate electrical energy.

- Nuclear fusion occurs when two or more nuclei combine to form a larger nucleus. The sun's energy comes from the fusion of hydrogen to form helium.

- The energy released by nuclear fission and nuclear fusion is produced when matter is converted into energy.

- Nuclear power plants use nuclear fission to supply many homes with electrical energy without releasing carbon dioxide or other gases into the atmosphere. A limited fuel supply, radioactive waste products, and the possible release of radioactive material are disadvantages of fission.

- Fuel for nuclear fusion is plentiful, and only small amounts of radioactive waste products are produced. Fusion is not currently a practical energy source because of the large amount of energy needed to heat and contain the hydrogen plasma.

 internet**connect**

GO TO: go.hrw.com

Visit the **HRW** Web site for a variety of learning tools related to this chapter. Just type in the keyword:

KEYWORD: HSTRAD

SCiLINKS SM

N S T A

GO TO: www.scilinks.org

Visit the **National Science Teachers Association** on-line Web site for Internet resources related to this chapter. Just type in the *sci*LINKS number for more information about the topic:

TOPIC:		**sciLINKS NUMBER:**
TOPIC: Discovering Radioactivity		**sciLINKS NUMBER:** HSTP380
TOPIC: Radioactive Isotopes		**sciLINKS NUMBER:** HSTP385
TOPIC: Nuclear Fission		**sciLINKS NUMBER:** HSTP390
TOPIC: Nuclear Reactors		**sciLINKS NUMBER:** HSTP395
TOPIC: Nuclear Fusion		**sciLINKS NUMBER:** HSTP400

Chapter Review

The statements below are false. For each statement, replace the underlined term to make a true statement.

1. <u>Nuclear fusion</u> involves splitting a nucleus.

2. During one <u>beta decay</u>, half of a radioactive sample will decay.

3. <u>Nuclear fission</u> includes the particles and rays released by radioactive nuclei.

4. <u>Alpha decay</u> occurs during the rearrangement of protons and neutrons in the nucleus.

UNDERSTANDING CONCEPTS

Multiple Choice

5. Which of the following is a use of radioactive material?
   a. detecting smoke
   b. locating defects in materials
   c. generating electrical energy
   d. all of the above

6. Which particle both begins and is produced by a nuclear chain reaction?
   a. positron
   b. neutron
   c. alpha particle
   d. beta particle

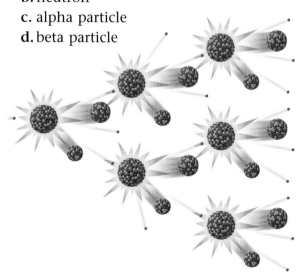

7. Nuclear radiation that can be stopped by paper is called
   a. alpha particles.   c. gamma rays.
   b. beta particles.   d. None of the above

8. The half-life of a radioactive atom is 2 months. If you start with 1g of the element, how much will remain after 6 months?
   a. One-half of a gram will remain.
   b. One-fourth of a gram will remain.
   c. One-eighth of a gram will remain.
   d. None will remain.

9. The waste products of nuclear fission
   a. are harmless.
   b. are safe after 20 years.
   c. can be destroyed by burning them.
   d. remain radioactive for thousands of years.

10. Which statement about nuclear fusion is false?
   a. Nuclear fusion occurs in the sun.
   b. Nuclear fusion is the joining of the nuclei of atoms.
   c. Nuclear fusion is currently used to generate electrical energy.
   d. Nuclear fusion uses hydrogen as fuel.

Short Answer

11. What conditions could cause a nucleus to be unstable?

12. What are two dangers associated with nuclear fission?

13. What are two of the problems that need to be solved in order to make nuclear fusion a practical energy source?

14. In fission, the products have less mass than the starting materials. Explain what happened.

Concept Mapping

15. Use the following terms to create a concept map: radioactive decay, alpha particle, beta particle, gamma ray, nuclear radiation.

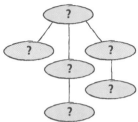

CRITICAL THINKING AND PROBLEM SOLVING

16. Smoke detectors often use americium-243 to detect smoke particles in the air. Americium-243 undergoes alpha decay. Do you think that these smoke detectors are safe to have in your home if used properly? Explain. (Hint: How penetrating are alpha particles?)

17. Explain how radiation can cause cancer.

18. Explain why nuclei of carbon, oxygen, and even iron can be found in stars.

19. If you could block all radiation from sources outside your body, explain why you would still be exposed to some radiation.

MATH IN SCIENCE

20. A scientist used 10 g of phosphorus-32 in a test on plant growth but forgot to record the date. When he measured the phosphorus-32 some time later, he found only 2.5 g remaining. If the half-life is 14 days, how many days ago did he start the experiment?

INTERPRETING GRAPHICS

21. Use the graph to answer the questions below:

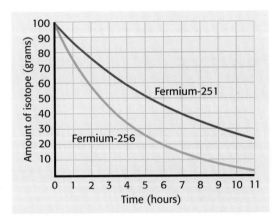

a. What is the half-life of fermium-256? of fermium-251?

b. Which of these isotopes is more stable? Explain.

22. The image of a small purse, shown below, was made in a similar manner as Becquerel's original experiment. What conclusions can be drawn about the penetrating power of radiation from this image?

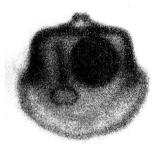

Reading Check-up

Take a minute to review your answers to the Pre-Reading Questions found at the bottom of page 78. Have your answers changed? If necessary, revise your answers based on what you have learned since you began this chapter.

Wasting Yucca Mountain?

Isolated, unspoiled, quiet . . . a small mountain in Nevada called Yucca Mountain seems like a perfect spot for a long hike—or perhaps a nuclear waste site! Yucca Mountain has been chosen as the nation's first storage site for high-level radioactive waste. The plan is to seal 77,000 tons of radioactive waste in steel canisters and store them in a maze of underground tunnels.

Construction of the facility has already begun—Yucca Mountain is scheduled to receive its first shipment of nuclear waste by 2010. But the debate continues about

▲ *Spent fuel rods are stored underwater at a nuclear power plant.*

Pros and Cons

Those who support construction of the Yucca Mountain facility point out that there are two major advantages to the plan. First, Yucca Mountain is far from any densely populated areas. Second, the climate is extremely dry. A dry climate means that rainfall is unlikely to cause the water table to rise and come in contact with the stored radioactive waste.

Many opponents fear that the highly toxic waste could eventually leak and contaminate the water in wells, springs, and streams. In time, the

whether it would be safer to store radioactive waste at Yucca Mountain or to keep it where it is now—in temporary storage facilities at various nuclear power plants.

contamination could spread farther from the site and into the biosphere. The biosphere is the layer above and below the surface of the earth that supports life.

In addition, some scientific reports suggest that it is possible that the current dry climate could change over thousands of years into a rainy one, and the water table could rise dramatically.

Nevada residents argue that their economy is booming and they don't particularly need the construction jobs the facility would bring. Also their economy depends heavily on tourism, and residents worry that fears about Nevada being a dangerous place could cause the tourists to stay away.

Today construction at the Yucca Mountain facility continues. And existing storage sites expand with the waste generated by nuclear power plants. So, where should the waste go?

Have Waste, Will Travel

▶ What do you think? Jot down your initial thoughts. Then do research to find out whether any of the proposed routes from nuclear power plants to Yucca Mountain are near your town. Do your findings change your opinion? Why or why not?

▲ *Supporters of the Yucca Mountain storage facility think that this isolated spot in Nevada is a suitable place for permanent nuclear-waste disposal. Opponents of the site disagree.*

CAREERS

MATERIALS SCIENTIST

Have you noticed that your forks, knives, and spoons don't tarnish easily? Most metal flatware is made of stainless steel. Because it doesn't tarnish easily, stainless steel is also used in nuclear reactors. **Dr. Michael Atzmon** studies radiation's effects on metals and other substances. He has a special interest in radiation's effect on stainless steel. He hopes that by understanding the changes that occur, scientists can prevent future radiation defects.

The damage to stainless steel is caused mainly by neutron and heavy ion radiation inside nuclear reactors. The radiation causes stress in the metal, which leads to corrosion and finally to cracking. Clearly this is not a desirable feature in parts of a nuclear reactor! Atzmon's goal is to try to understand how to make the metal more corrosion resistant. He also hopes that by studying the way radiation affects the atoms of metals, he can find a way to use the incoming radiation to make the surface stronger.

Training the Team

A large part of Atzmon's job is to train graduate students to assist him with his research. He happily reports that these creative new scientists "absolutely contribute" to the development of novel approaches. One interesting proposal is to use radiation effects to create crystal structures different from those that exist in nature. This could lead to the invention of new types of semiconductors, which are useful in modern electronic devices.

Always an Explorer

Atzmon spends time sharing ideas with other materials scientists. He also teaches at the University of Michigan. This very busy man recalls that as a young boy he became interested in experimenting with things to see how they work. He chose to play with toys that encouraged his exploration. This curiosity has remained with him and has been helpful in his profession.

▶ *Understanding material structures can help in the development of better semiconductors for microchips.*

Advice to Young People

Atzmon believes that students should choose to study a field that gives them the deepest background. This opens up many career opportunities and allows students to pursue what they eventually find interesting. Most important, he adds, "People should do what they love doing!"

Exploring, inventing, and investigating are essential to the study of science. However, these activities can also be dangerous. To make sure that your experiments and explorations are safe, you must be aware of a variety of safety guidelines.

You have probably heard of the saying, "It is better to be safe than sorry." This is particularly true in a science classroom where experiments and explorations are being performed. Being uninformed and careless can result in serious injuries. Don't take chances with your own safety or with anyone else's.

Following are important guidelines for staying safe in the science classroom. Your teacher may also have safety guidelines and tips that are specific to your classroom and laboratory. Take the time to be safe.

Safety Rules!

Start Out Right

Always get your teacher's permission before attempting any laboratory exploration. Read the procedures carefully, and pay particular attention to safety information and caution statements. If you are unsure about what a safety symbol means, look it up or ask your teacher. You cannot be too careful when it comes to safety. If an accident does occur, inform your teacher immediately, regardless of how minor you think the accident is.

Safety Symbols

All of the experiments and investigations in this book and their related worksheets include important safety symbols to alert you to particular safety concerns. Become familiar with these symbols so that when you see them, you will know what they mean and what to do. It is important that you read this entire safety section to learn about specific dangers in the laboratory.

If you are instructed to note the odor of a substance, wave the fumes toward your nose with your hand. Never put your nose close to the source.

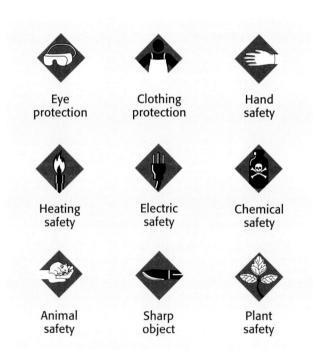

Eye protection

Clothing protection

Hand safety

Heating safety

Electric safety

Chemical safety

Animal safety

Sharp object

Plant safety

Eye Safety

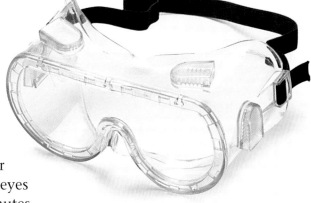

Wear safety goggles when working around chemicals, acids, bases, or any type of flame or heating device. Wear safety goggles any time there is even the slightest chance that harm could come to your eyes. If any substance gets into your eyes, notify your teacher immediately, and flush your eyes with running water for at least 15 minutes. Treat any unknown chemical as if it were a dangerous chemical. Never look directly into the sun. Doing so could cause permanent blindness.

Avoid wearing contact lenses in a laboratory situation. Even if you are wearing safety goggles, chemicals can get between the contact lenses and your eyes. If your doctor requires that you wear contact lenses instead of glasses, wear eye-cup safety goggles in the lab.

Safety Equipment

Know the locations of the nearest fire alarms and any other safety equipment, such as fire blankets and eyewash fountains, as identified by your teacher, and know the procedures for using them.

Be extra careful when using any glassware. When adding a heavy object to a graduated cylinder, tilt the cylinder so the object slides slowly to the bottom.

Neatness

Keep your work area free of all unnecessary books and papers. Tie back long hair, and secure loose sleeves or other loose articles of clothing, such as ties and bows. Remove dangling jewelry. Don't wear open-toed shoes or sandals in the laboratory. Never eat, drink, or apply cosmetics in a laboratory setting. Food, drink, and cosmetics can easily become contaminated with dangerous materials.

Certain hair products (such as aerosol hair spray) are flammable and should not be worn while working near an open flame. Avoid wearing hair spray or hair gel on lab days.

Sharp/Pointed Objects

Use knives and other sharp instruments with extreme care. Never cut objects while holding them in your hands. Place objects on a suitable work surface for cutting.

Heat

Wear safety goggles when using a heating device or a flame. Whenever possible, use an electric hot plate as a heat source instead of an open flame. When heating materials in a test tube, always angle the test tube away from yourself and others. In order to avoid burns, wear heat-resistant gloves whenever instructed to do so.

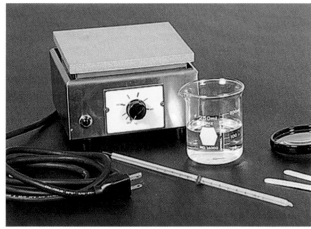

Electricity

Be careful with electrical cords. When using a microscope with a lamp, do not place the cord where it could trip someone. Do not let cords hang over a table edge in a way that could cause equipment to fall if the cord is accidentally pulled. Do not use equipment with damaged cords. Be sure your hands are dry and that the electrical equipment is in the "off" position before plugging it in. Turn off and unplug electrical equipment when you are finished.

Chemicals

Wear safety goggles when handling any potentially dangerous chemicals, acids, or bases. If a chemical is unknown, handle it as you would a dangerous chemical. Wear an apron and safety gloves when working with acids or bases or whenever you are told to do so. If a spill gets on your skin or clothing, rinse it off immediately with water for at least 5 minutes while calling to your teacher.

Never mix chemicals unless your teacher tells you to do so. Never taste, touch, or smell chemicals unless you are specifically directed to do so. Before working with a flammable liquid or gas, check for the presence of any source of flame, spark, or heat.

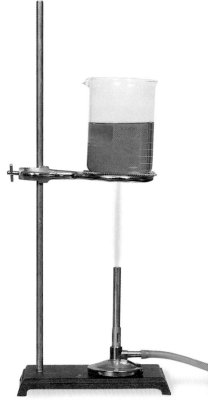

Animal Safety

Always obtain your teacher's permission before bringing any animal into the school building. Handle animals only as your teacher directs. Always treat animals carefully and with respect. Wash your hands thoroughly after handling any animal.

Plant Safety

Do not eat any part of a plant or plant seed used in the laboratory. Wash hands thoroughly after handling any part of a plant. When in nature, do not pick any wild plants unless your teacher instructs you to do so.

Glassware

Examine all glassware before use. Be sure that glassware is clean and free of chips and cracks. Report damaged glassware to your teacher. Glass containers used for heating should be made of heat-resistant glass.

Finding a Balance

Usually, balancing a chemical equation involves just writing in your ScienceLog. But in this activity, you will use models to practice balancing chemical equations, as shown below. By following the rules, you will soon become an expert equation balancer!

Materials

- envelopes, each labeled with an unbalanced equation

Example

$$\_H_2 + \_O_2 \rightarrow \_H_2O$$

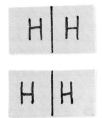  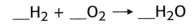 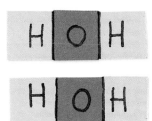

Balanced Equation

$$2H_2 + O_2 \rightarrow 2H_2O$$

Procedure

1. The rules:
   a. Reactant-molecule models may be placed only to the left of the arrow.
   b. Product-molecule models may be placed only to the right of the arrow.
   c. You may use only complete molecule models.
   d. At least one of each of the reactant and product molecules shown in the equation must be included in the model when you are finished.

2. Select one of the labeled envelopes. Copy the unbalanced equation written on the envelope into your ScienceLog.

3. Open the envelope, and pull out the molecule models and the arrow. Place the arrow in the center of your work area.

4. Put one model of each molecule that is a reactant on the left side of the arrow and one model of each product on the right side.

5. Add one reactant-molecule or product-molecule model at a time until the number of each of the different-colored squares on each side of the arrow is the same. Remember to follow the rules.

6. When the equation is balanced, count the number of each of the molecule models you used. Write these numbers as coefficients, as shown in the balanced equation above.

7. Select another envelope, and repeat the steps until you have balanced all of the equations.

Analysis

8. The rules specify that you are only allowed to use complete molecule models. How is this similar to what occurs in a real chemical reaction?

9. In chemical reactions, energy is either released or absorbed. In your ScienceLog, devise a way to improve the model to show energy being released or absorbed.

DISCOVERY LAB

Cata-what? Catalyst!

Catalysts increase the rate of a chemical reaction without being changed during the reaction. In this experiment, hydrogen peroxide, H_2O_2, decomposes into oxygen, O_2, and water, H_2O. An enzyme present in liver cells acts as a catalyst for this reaction. You will investigate the relationship between the amount of the catalyst and the rate of the decomposition reaction.

Ask a Question

1. How does the amount of a catalyst affect reaction rate?

Form a Hypothesis

2. In your ScienceLog, write a statement that answers the question above. Explain your reasoning.

Test the Hypothesis

3. Put a small piece of masking tape near the top of each test tube, and label the tubes 1, 2, and 3.

4. Create a hot-water bath by filling the beaker half-full with hot water.

5. Using the funnel and graduated cylinder, measure 5 mL of the hydrogen peroxide solution into each test tube. Place the test tubes in the hot-water bath for 5 minutes.

6. While the test tubes warm up, grind one liver cube with the mortar and pestle.

7. After 5 minutes, use the tweezers to place the cube of liver in test tube 1. Place the ground liver in test tube 2. Leave test tube 3 alone.

Make Observations

8. Observe the reaction rate (the amount of bubbling) in all three test tubes, and record your observations in your ScienceLog.

Materials

- 10 mL test tubes (3)
- masking tape
- 600 mL beaker
- hot water
- funnel
- 10 mL graduated cylinder
- hydrogen peroxide solution
- 2 small liver cubes
- mortar and pestle
- tweezers

Analyze Your Results

9. Does liver appear to be a catalyst? Explain your answer.

10. Which type of liver (whole or ground) produced a faster reaction? Why?

11. What is the purpose of test tube 3?

Draw Conclusions

12. How do your results support or disprove your hypothesis?

13. Why was a hot-water bath used? (Hint: Look in your book for a definition of activation energy.)

DISCOVERY LAB

Speed Control

The reaction rate (how fast a chemical reaction happens) is an important factor to control. Sometimes you want a reaction to take place rapidly, such as when you are removing tarnish from a metal surface. Other times you want a reaction to happen very slowly, such as when you are depending on a battery as a source of electrical energy. In this lab, you will discover how changing the surface area and concentration of the reactants affects reaction rate. In this lab, you can estimate the rate of reaction by observing how fast bubbles form.

Materials

- 30 mL test tubes (6)
- 6 strips of aluminum, approximately 5 × 1 cm each
- test-tube rack
- scissors
- 2 funnels
- 10 mL graduated cylinders (2)
- acid A
- acid B

Part A—Surface Area

Ask a Question

1. How does changing the surface area of a metal affect reaction rate?

Form a Hypothesis

2. In your ScienceLog, write a statement that answers the question above. Explain your reasoning.

Test the Hypothesis

3. Use three identical strips of aluminum. Put one strip into a test tube. Place the test tube in the test-tube rack.
   Caution: The strips of metal may have sharp edges.

4. Carefully fold a second strip in half and then in half again. Use a text book or other large object to flatten the folded strip as much as possible. Place the strip in a second test tube in the test-tube rack.

5. Use scissors to cut a third strip of aluminum into the smallest possible pieces. Place all of the pieces into a third test tube, and place the test tube in the test-tube rack.

6. Use a funnel and a graduated cylinder to pour 10 mL of acid A into each of the three test tubes.
   Caution: Hydrochloric acid is corrosive. If any acid should spill on you, immediately flush the area with water and notify your teacher.

Make Observations

7. Observe the rate of bubble formation in each test tube. Record your observations in your ScienceLog.

Analyze the Results

8. Which form of aluminum had the greatest surface area? Which had the smallest?

9. In the three test tubes, the amount of aluminum and the amount of acid were the same. Which form of the aluminum seemed to react the fastest? Which form reacted the slowest? Explain your answers.

10. Do your results support the hypothesis you made in step 2? Explain.

Draw Conclusions

11. Would powdered aluminum react faster or slower than the forms of aluminum you used? Explain your answer.

Part B—Concentration

Ask a Question

12. How does changing the concentration of acid affect the reaction rate?

Form a Hypothesis

13. In your ScienceLog, write a statement that answers the question above. Explain your reasoning.

Test the Hypothesis

14. Place one of the three remaining aluminum strips in each of the three clean test tubes. (Note: Do not alter the strips.) Place the test tubes in the test-tube rack.

15. Using the second funnel and graduated cylinder, pour 10 mL of water into one of the test tubes. Pour 10 mL of acid B into the second test tube. Pour 10 mL of acid A into the third test tube.

Make Observations

16. Observe the rate of bubble formation in the three test tubes. Record your observations in your ScienceLog.

Analyze the Results

17. In this set of test tubes, the strips of aluminum were the same, but the concentration of the acid was different. Acid A is more concentrated than acid B. Was there a difference between the test tube with water and the test tubes with acid? Which test tube formed bubbles the fastest? Explain your answers.

18. Do your results support the hypothesis you made in step 13? Explain.

Draw Conclusions

19. Explain why spilled hydrochloric acid should be diluted with water before it is wiped up.

Making Salt

A neutralization reaction between an acid and a base produces water and a salt. In this lab, you will react an acid with a base and then let the water evaporate. You will then examine what is left for properties that tell you that it is indeed a salt.

Materials

- hydrochloric acid
- 100 mL graduated cylinder
- 100 mL beaker
- distilled water
- phenolphthalein solution in a dropper bottle
- sodium hydroxide
- glass stirring rod
- 2 eyedroppers
- evaporating dish
- magnifying lens

Procedure

1. Put on protective gloves. Carefully measure 25 mL of hydrochloric acid in a graduated cylinder, then pour it into the beaker. Carefully rinse the graduated cylinder with distilled water to clean out any leftover acid.
   Caution: Hydrochloric acid is corrosive. If any should spill on you, immediately flush the area with water and notify your teacher.

2. Add three drops of phenolphthalein indicator to the acid in the beaker. You will not see anything happen yet because this indicator won't show its color unless too much base is present.

3. Measure 20 mL of sodium hydroxide (base) in the graduated cylinder, and add it slowly to the beaker with the acid. Use the stirring rod to mix the substances completely.
   Caution: Sodium hydroxide is also corrosive. If any should spill on you, immediately flush the area with water and notify your teacher.

4. Use an eyedropper to add more base to the acid-base mixture in the beaker a few drops at a time. Be sure to stir the mixture after each few drops. Continue adding drops of base until the mixture remains colored after stirring.

5. Use another eyedropper to add acid to the beaker, one drop at a time, until the color just disappears after stirring.

6. Pour the mixture carefully into an evaporating dish, and place the dish where your teacher tells you to allow the water to evaporate overnight.

7. The next day, examine your evaporating dish and study the crystals that were left with a magnifying lens. Identify the color, shape, and other properties that the crystals have.

Analysis

8. The equation for the reaction above is:

$$HCl + NaOH \longrightarrow H_2O + NaCl.$$

NaCl is ordinary table salt and forms very regular cubic crystals that are white. Did you find white cubic crystals?

9. The phenolphthalein indicator changes color in the presence of a base. Why did you add more acid in step 5 until the color disappeared?

Going Further

Another neutralization reaction occurs between hydrochloric acid and potassium hydroxide, KOH. The equation for this reaction is as follows:

$$HCl + KOH \longrightarrow H_2O + KCl$$

What are the products of this neutralization reaction? How do they compare with those you discovered in this experiment?

Concept Mapping: A Way to Bring Ideas Together

What Is a Concept Map?

Have you ever tried to tell someone about a book or a chapter you've just read and found that you can remember only a few isolated words and ideas? Or maybe you've memorized facts for a test and then weeks later discovered you're not even sure what topics those facts covered.

In both cases, you may have understood the ideas or concepts by themselves but not in relation to one another. If you could somehow link the ideas together, you would probably understand them better and remember them longer. This is something a concept map can help you do. A concept map is a way to see how ideas or concepts fit together. It can help you see the "big picture."

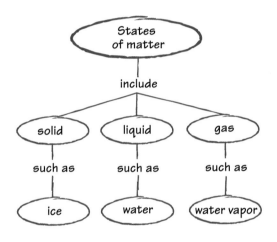

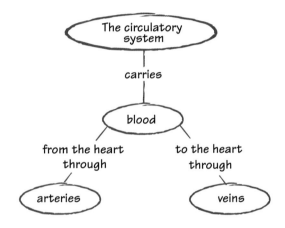

How to Make a Concept Map

❶ Make a list of the main ideas or concepts.

It might help to write each concept on its own slip of paper. This will make it easier to rearrange the concepts as many times as necessary to make sense of how the concepts are connected. After you've made a few concept maps this way, you can go directly from writing your list to actually making the map.

❷ Arrange the concepts in order from the most general to the most specific.

Put the most general concept at the top and circle it. Ask yourself, "How does this concept relate to the remaining concepts?" As you see the relationships, arrange the concepts in order from general to specific.

❸ Connect the related concepts with lines.

❹ On each line, write an action word or short phrase that shows how the concepts are related.

Look at the concept maps on this page, and then see if you can make one for the following terms:

plants, water, photosynthesis, carbon dioxide, sun's energy

One possible answer is provided at right, but don't look at it until you try the concept map yourself.

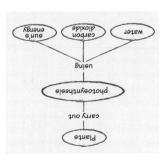

SI Measurement

The International System of Units, or SI, is the standard system of measurement used by many scientists. Using the same standards of measurement makes it easier for scientists to communicate with one another.

SI works by combining prefixes and base units. Each base unit can be used with different prefixes to define smaller and larger quantities. The table below lists common SI prefixes.

SI Prefixes			
Prefix	**Abbreviation**	**Factor**	**Example**
kilo-	k	1,000	kilogram, 1 kg = 1,000 g
hecto-	h	100	hectoliter, 1 hL = 100 L
deka-	da	10	dekameter, 1 dam = 10 m
		1	meter, liter
deci-	d	0.1	decigram, 1 dg = 0.1 g
centi-	c	0.01	centimeter, 1 cm = 0.01 m
milli-	m	0.001	milliliter, 1 mL = 0.001 L
micro-	μ	0.000 001	micrometer, 1 μm = 0.000 001 m

SI Conversion Table		
SI units	**From SI to English**	**From English to SI**
Length		
kilometer (km) = 1,000 m	1 km = 0.621 mi	1 mi = 1.609 km
meter (m) = 100 cm	1 m = 3.281 ft	1 ft = 0.305 m
centimeter (cm) = 0.01 m	1 cm = 0.394 in.	1 in. = 2.540 cm
millimeter (mm) = 0.001 m	1 mm = 0.039 in.	
micrometer (μm) = 0.000 001 m		
nanometer (nm) = 0.000 000 001 m		
Area		
square kilometer (km^2) = 100 hectares	1 km^2 = 0.386 mi^2	1 mi^2 = 2.590 km^2
hectare (ha) = 10,000 m^2	1 ha = 2.471 acres	1 acre = 0.405 ha
square meter (m^2) = 10,000 cm^2	1 m^2 = 10.765 ft^2	1 ft^2 = 0.093 m^2
square centimeter (cm^2) = 100 mm^2	1 cm^2 = 0.155 in.^{2}	1 in.^{2} = 6.452 cm^2
Volume		
liter (L) = 1,000 mL = 1 dm^3	1 L = 1.057 fl qt	1 fl qt = 0.946 L
milliliter (mL) = 0.001 L = 1 cm^3	1 mL = 0.034 fl oz	1 fl oz = 29.575 mL
microliter (μL) = 0.000 001 L		
Mass		
kilogram (kg) = 1,000 g	1 kg = 2.205 lb	1 lb = 0.454 kg
gram (g) = 1,000 mg	1 g = 0.035 oz	1 oz = 28.349 g
milligram (mg) = 0.001 g		
microgram (μg) = 0.000 001 g		

Temperature Scales

Temperature can be expressed using three different scales: Fahrenheit, Celsius, and Kelvin. The SI unit for temperature is the kelvin (K).

Although 0 K is much colder than 0°C, a change of 1 K is equal to a change of 1°C.

Three Temperature Scales

	Fahrenheit	Celsius	Kelvin
Water boils	212°	100°	373
Body temperature	98.6°	37°	310
Room temperature	68°	20°	293
Water freezes	32°	0°	273

Temperature Conversions Table

To convert	Use this equation:	Example
Celsius to Fahrenheit °C ⟶ °F	$°F = \left(\dfrac{9}{5} \times °C\right) + 32$	Convert 45°C to °F. $°F = \left(\dfrac{9}{5} \times 45°C\right) + 32 = 113°F$
Fahrenheit to Celsius °F ⟶ °C	$°C = \dfrac{5}{9} \times (°F - 32)$	Convert 68°F to °C. $°C = \dfrac{5}{9} \times (68°F - 32) = 20°C$
Celsius to Kelvin °C ⟶ K	$K = °C + 273$	Convert 45°C to K. $K = 45°C + 273 = 318\ K$
Kelvin to Celsius K ⟶ °C	$°C = K - 273$	Convert 32 K to °C. $°C = 32\ K - 273 = -241°C$

Measuring Skills

Using a Graduated Cylinder

When using a graduated cylinder to measure volume, keep the following procedures in mind:

① Make sure the cylinder is on a flat, level surface.

② Move your head so that your eye is level with the surface of the liquid.

③ Read the mark closest to the liquid level. On glass graduated cylinders, read the mark closest to the center of the curve in the liquid's surface.

Using a Meterstick or Metric Ruler

When using a meterstick or metric ruler to measure length, keep the following procedures in mind:

① Place the ruler firmly against the object you are measuring.

② Align one edge of the object exactly with the zero end of the ruler.

③ Look at the other edge of the object to see which of the marks on the ruler is closest to that edge. **Note:** Each small slash between the centimeters represents a millimeter, which is one-tenth of a centimeter.

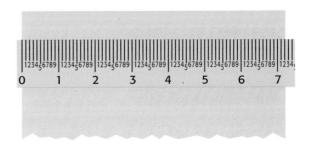

Using a Triple-Beam Balance

When using a triple-beam balance to measure mass, keep the following procedures in mind:

① Make sure the balance is on a level surface.

② Place all of the countermasses at zero. Adjust the balancing knob until the pointer rests at zero.

③ Place the object you wish to measure on the pan. **Caution:** Do not place hot objects or chemicals directly on the balance pan.

④ Move the largest countermass along the beam to the right until it is at the last notch that does not tip the balance. Follow the same procedure with the next-largest countermass. Then move the smallest countermass until the pointer rests at zero.

⑤ Add the readings from the three beams together to determine the mass of the object.

⑥ When determining the mass of crystals or powders, use a piece of filter paper. First find the mass of the paper. Then add the crystals or powder to the paper and re-measure. The actual mass of the crystals or powder is the total mass minus the mass of the paper. When finding the mass of liquids, first find the mass of the empty container. Then find the mass of the liquid and container together. The mass of the liquid is the total mass minus the mass of the container.

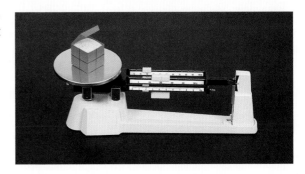

Scientific Method

The series of steps that scientists use to answer questions and solve problems is often called the **scientific method.** The scientific method is not a rigid procedure. Scientists may use all of the steps or just some of the steps of the scientific method. They may even repeat some of the steps. The goal of the scientific method is to come up with reliable answers and solutions.

Six Steps of the Scientific Method

1 **Ask a Question** Good questions come from careful **observations.** You make observations by using your senses to gather information. Sometimes you may use instruments, such as microscopes and telescopes, to extend the range of your senses. As you observe the natural world, you will discover that you have many more questions than answers. These questions drive the scientific method.

Questions beginning with *what, why, how,* and *when* are very important in focusing an investigation, and they often lead to a hypothesis. (You will learn what a hypothesis is in the next step.) Here is an example of a question that could lead to further investigation.

Question: How does acid rain affect plant growth?

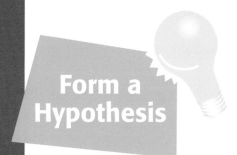

2 **Form a Hypothesis** After you come up with a question, you need to turn the question into a **hypothesis.** A hypothesis is a clear statement of what you expect the answer to your question to be. Your hypothesis will represent your best "educated guess" based on your observations and what you already know. A good hypothesis is testable. If observations and information cannot be gathered or if an experiment cannot be designed to test your hypothesis, it is untestable, and the investigation can go no further.

Here is a hypothesis that could be formed from the question, "How does acid rain affect plant growth?"

Hypothesis: Acid rain causes plants to grow more slowly.

Notice that the hypothesis provides some specifics that lead to methods of testing. The hypothesis can also lead to predictions. A **prediction** is what you think will be the outcome of your experiment or data collection. Predictions are usually stated in an "if . . . then" format. For example, **if** meat is kept at room temperature, **then** it will spoil faster than meat kept in the refrigerator. More than one prediction can be made for a single hypothesis. Here is a sample prediction for the hypothesis that acid rain causes plants to grow more slowly.

Prediction: If a plant is watered with only acid rain (which has a pH of 4), then the plant will grow at half its normal rate.

3 **Test the Hypothesis** After you have formed a hypothesis and made a prediction, you should test your hypothesis. There are different ways to do this. Perhaps the most familiar way is to conduct a **controlled experiment.** A controlled experiment tests only one factor at a time. A controlled experiment has a **control group** and one or more **experimental groups.** All the factors for the control and experimental groups are the same except for one factor, which is called the **variable.** By changing only one factor, you can see the results of just that one change.

Sometimes, the nature of an investigation makes a controlled experiment impossible. For example, dinosaurs have been extinct for millions of years, and the Earth's core is surrounded by thousands of meters of rock. It would be difficult, if not impossible, to conduct controlled experiments on such things. Under such circumstances, a hypothesis may be tested by making detailed observations. Taking measurements is one way of making observations.

Test the Hypothesis

4 **Analyze the Results** After you have completed your experiments, made your observations, and collected your data, you must analyze all the information you have gathered. Tables and graphs are often used in this step to organize the data.

Analyze the Results

5 **Draw Conclusions** Based on the analysis of your data, you should conclude whether or not your results support your hypothesis. If your hypothesis is supported, you (or others) might want to repeat the observations or experiments to verify your results. If your hypothesis is not supported by the data, you may have to check your procedure for errors. You may even have to reject your hypothesis and make a new one. If you cannot draw a conclusion from your results, you may have to try the investigation again or carry out further observations or experiments.

Draw Conclusions

Do they support your hypothesis?

No

Yes

6 **Communicate Results** After any scientific investigation, you should report your results. By doing a written or oral report, you let others know what you have learned. They may want to repeat your investigation to see if they get the same results. Your report may even lead to another question, which in turn may lead to another investigation.

Communicate Results

Scientific Method in Action

The scientific method is not a "straight line" of steps. It contains loops in which several steps may be repeated over and over again, while others may not be necessary. For example, sometimes scientists will find that testing one hypothesis raises new questions and new hypotheses to be tested. And sometimes, testing the hypothesis leads directly to a conclusion. Furthermore, the steps in the scientific method are not always used in the same order. Follow the steps in the diagram below, and see how many different directions the scientific method can take you.

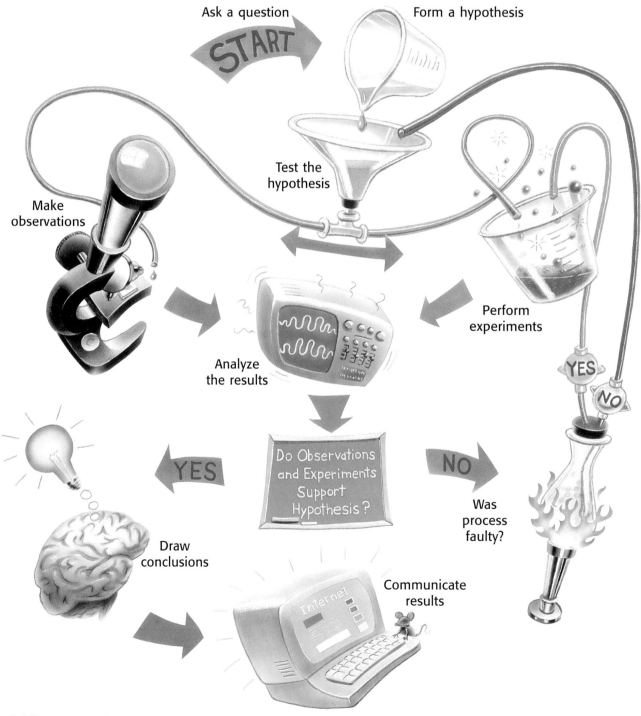

Ask a question

START

Form a hypothesis

Test the hypothesis

Make observations

Perform experiments

YES

NO

Analyze the results

Do Observations and Experiments Support Hypothesis?

YES

NO

Was process faulty?

Draw conclusions

Communicate results

Internet

Making Charts and Graphs

Circle Graphs

A circle graph, or pie chart, shows how each group of data relates to all of the data. Each part of the circle represents a category of the data. The entire circle represents all of the data. For example, a biologist studying a hardwood forest in Wisconsin found that there were five different types of trees. The data table at right summarizes the biologist's findings.

Wisconsin Hardwood Trees	
Type of tree	**Number found**
Oak	600
Maple	750
Beech	300
Birch	1,200
Hickory	150
Total	3,000

How to Make a Circle Graph

1 In order to make a circle graph of this data, first find the percentage of each type of tree. To do this, divide the number of individual trees by the total number of trees and multiply by 100.

$$\frac{600 \text{ oak}}{3,000 \text{ trees}} \times 100 = 20\%$$

$$\frac{750 \text{ maple}}{3,000 \text{ trees}} \times 100 = 25\%$$

$$\frac{300 \text{ beech}}{3,000 \text{ trees}} \times 100 = 10\%$$

$$\frac{1,200 \text{ birch}}{3,000 \text{ trees}} \times 100 = 40\%$$

$$\frac{150 \text{ hickory}}{3,000 \text{ trees}} \times 100 = 5\%$$

2 Now determine the size of the pie shapes that make up the chart. Do this by multiplying each percentage by 360°. Remember that a circle contains 360°.

$20\% \times 360° = 72°$ $25\% \times 360° = 90°$
$10\% \times 360° = 36°$ $40\% \times 360° = 144°$
$5\% \times 360° = 18°$

3 Then check that the sum of the percentages is 100 and the sum of the degrees is 360.

$20\% + 25\% + 10\% + 40\% + 5\% = 100\%$
$72° + 90° + 36° + 144° + 18° = 360°$

4 Use a compass to draw a circle and mark its center.

5 Then use a protractor to draw angles of 72°, 90°, 36°, 144°, and 18° in the circle.

6 Finally, label each part of the graph, and choose an appropriate title.

A Community of Wisconsin Hardwood Trees

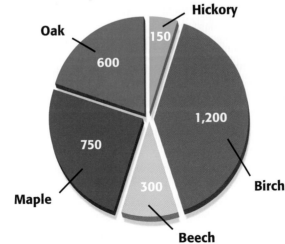

Line Graphs

Line graphs are most often used to demonstrate continuous change. For example, Mr. Smith's science class analyzed the population records for their hometown, Appleton, between 1900 and 2000. Examine the data at left.

Because the year and the population change, they are the *variables*. The population is determined by, or dependent on, the year. Therefore, the population is called the **dependent variable**, and the year is called the **independent variable**. Each set of data is called a **data pair**. To prepare a line graph, data pairs must first be organized in a table like the one at left.

Population of Appleton, 1900–2000	
Year	Population
1900	1,800
1920	2,500
1940	3,200
1960	3,900
1980	4,600
2000	5,300

How to Make a Line Graph

1 Place the independent variable along the horizontal (*x*) axis. Place the dependent variable along the vertical (*y*) axis.

2 Label the *x*-axis "Year" and the *y*-axis "Population." Look at your largest and smallest values for the population. Determine a scale for the *y*-axis that will provide enough space to show these values. You must use the same scale for the entire length of the axis. Find an appropriate scale for the *x*-axis too.

3 Choose reasonable starting points for each axis.

4 Plot the data pairs as accurately as possible.

5 Choose a title that accurately represents the data.

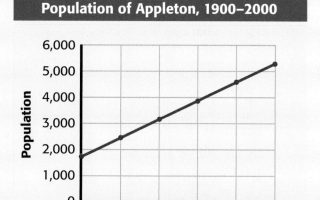

Population of Appleton, 1900–2000

How to Determine Slope

Slope is the ratio of the change in the *y*-axis to the change in the *x*-axis, or "rise over run."

1 Choose two points on the line graph. For example, the population of Appleton in 2000 was 5,300 people. Therefore, you can define point *a* as (2000, 5,300). In 1900, the population was 1,800 people. Define point *b* as (1900, 1,800).

2 Find the change in the *y*-axis. (*y* at point *a*) − (*y* at point *b*) 5,300 people − 1,800 people = 3,500 people

3 Find the change in the *x*-axis. (*x* at point *a*) − (*x* at point *b*) 2000 − 1900 = 100 years

4 Calculate the slope of the graph by dividing the change in *y* by the change in *x*.

$$\text{slope} = \frac{\text{change in } y}{\text{change in } x}$$

$$\text{slope} = \frac{3{,}500 \text{ people}}{100 \text{ years}}$$

$$\text{slope} = 35 \text{ people per year}$$

In this example, the population in Appleton increased by a fixed amount each year. The graph of this data is a straight line. Therefore, the relationship is **linear**. When the graph of a set of data is not a straight line, the relationship is **nonlinear**.

Using Algebra to Determine Slope

The equation in step 4 may also be arranged to be:

$$y = kx$$

where y represents the change in the y-axis, k represents the slope, and x represents the change in the x-axis.

$$slope = \frac{change\ in\ y}{change\ in\ x}$$

$$k = \frac{y}{x}$$

$$k \times x = \frac{y \times x}{x}$$

$$kx = y$$

Bar Graphs

Bar graphs are used to demonstrate change that is not continuous. These graphs can be used to indicate trends when the data are taken over a long period of time. A meteorologist gathered the precipitation records at right for Hartford, Connecticut, for April 1–15, 1996, and used a bar graph to represent the data.

Precipitation in Hartford, Connecticut April 1–15, 1996

Date	Precipitation (cm)	Date	Precipitation (cm)
April 1	0.5	April 9	0.25
April 2	1.25	April 10	0.0
April 3	0.0	April 11	1.0
April 4	0.0	April 12	0.0
April 5	0.0	April 13	0.25
April 6	0.0	April 14	0.0
April 7	0.0	April 15	6.50
April 8	1.75		

How to Make a Bar Graph

1 Use an appropriate scale and a reasonable starting point for each axis.

2 Label the axes, and plot the data.

3 Choose a title that accurately represents the data.

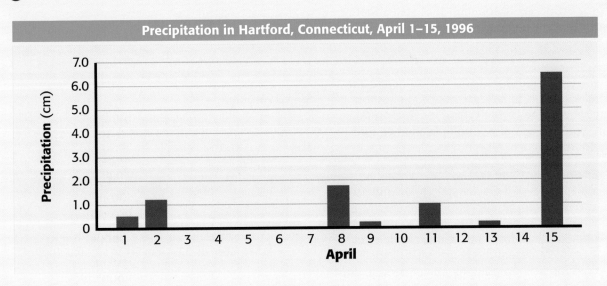

Precipitation in Hartford, Connecticut, April 1–15, 1996

Math Refresher

Science requires an understanding of many math concepts. The following pages will help you review some important math skills.

Averages

An **average,** or **mean,** simplifies a list of numbers into a single number that *approximates* their value.

> **Example:** Find the average of the following set of numbers: 5, 4, 7, and 8.

Step 1: Find the sum.

$$5 + 4 + 7 + 8 = 24$$

Step 2: Divide the sum by the amount of numbers in your set. Because there are four numbers in this example, divide the sum by 4.

$$\frac{24}{4} = 6$$

The average, or mean, is **6.**

Ratios

A **ratio** is a comparison between numbers, and it is usually written as a fraction.

> **Example:** Find the ratio of thermometers to students if you have 36 thermometers and 48 students in your class.

Step 1: Make the ratio.

$$\frac{36 \text{ thermometers}}{48 \text{ students}}$$

Step 2: Reduce the fraction to its simplest form.

$$\frac{36}{48} = \frac{36 \div 12}{48 \div 12} = \frac{3}{4}$$

The ratio of thermometers to students is **3 to 4,** or $\frac{3}{4}$. The ratio may also be written in the form 3:4.

Proportions

A **proportion** is an equation that states that two ratios are equal.

$$\frac{3}{1} = \frac{12}{4}$$

To solve a proportion, first multiply across the equal sign. This is called cross-multiplication. If you know three of the quantities in a proportion, you can use cross-multiplication to find the fourth.

> **Example:** Imagine that you are making a scale model of the solar system for your science project. The diameter of Jupiter is 11.2 times the diameter of the Earth. If you are using a plastic-foam ball with a diameter of 2 cm to represent the Earth, what diameter does the ball representing Jupiter need to be?
>
> $$\frac{11.2}{1} = \frac{x}{2 \text{ cm}}$$

Step 1: Cross-multiply.

$$\frac{11.2}{1} \diagdown \frac{x}{2}$$

$$11.2 \times 2 = x \times 1$$

Step 2: Multiply.

$$22.4 = x \times 1$$

Step 3: Isolate the variable by dividing both sides by 1.

$$x = \frac{22.4}{1}$$
$$x = 22.4 \text{ cm}$$

You will need to use a ball with a diameter of **22.4 cm** to represent Jupiter.

Percentages

A **percentage** is a ratio of a given number to 100.

Example: What is 85 percent of 40?

Step 1: Rewrite the percentage by moving the decimal point two places to the left.

$$.85$$

Step 2: Multiply the decimal by the number you are calculating the percentage of.

$$0.85 \times 40 = 34$$

85 percent of 40 is **34.**

Decimals

To **add** or **subtract decimals,** line up the digits vertically so that the decimal points line up. Then add or subtract the columns from right to left, carrying or borrowing numbers as necessary.

Example: Add the following numbers: 3.1415 and 2.96.

Step 1: Line up the digits vertically so that the decimal points line up.

$$
\begin{array}{r}
3.1415 \\
+ \ 2.96 \\
\hline
\end{array}
$$

Step 2: Add the columns from right to left, carrying when necessary.

$$
\begin{array}{r}
1 \ 1 \\
3.1415 \\
+ \ 2.96 \\
\hline
6.1015
\end{array}
$$

The sum is **6.1015.**

Fractions

Numbers tell you how many; **fractions** tell you *how much of a whole.*

Example: Your class has 24 plants. Your teacher instructs you to put 5 in a shady spot. What fraction does this represent?

Step 1: Write a fraction with the total number of parts in the whole as the denominator.

$$\frac{?}{24}$$

Step 2: Write the number of parts of the whole being represented as the numerator.

$$\frac{5}{24}$$

$\frac{5}{24}$ of the plants will be in the shade.

Reducing Fractions

It is usually best to express a fraction in simplest form. This is called *reducing* a fraction.

Example: Reduce the fraction $\frac{30}{45}$ to its simplest form.

Step 1: Find the largest whole number that will divide evenly into both the numerator and denominator. This number is called the greatest common factor (GCF).

factors of the numerator 30: 1, 2, 3, 5, 6, 10, **15,** 30

factors of the denominator 45: 1, 3, 5, 9, **15,** 45

Step 2: Divide both the numerator and the denominator by the GCF, which in this case is 15.

$$\frac{30}{45} = \frac{30 \div 15}{45 \div 15} = \frac{2}{3}$$

$\frac{30}{45}$ reduced to its simplest form is $\frac{2}{3}$.

Adding and Subtracting Fractions

To **add** or **subtract fractions** that have the **same denominator,** simply add or subtract the numerators.

Examples:

$$\frac{3}{5} + \frac{1}{5} = ? \text{ and } \frac{3}{4} - \frac{1}{4} = ?$$

Step 1: Add or subtract the numerators.

$$\frac{3}{5} + \frac{1}{5} = \frac{4}{} \text{ and } \frac{3}{4} - \frac{1}{4} = \frac{2}{}$$

Step 2: Write the sum or difference over the denominator.

$$\frac{3}{5} + \frac{1}{5} = \frac{4}{5} \text{ and } \frac{3}{4} - \frac{1}{4} = \frac{2}{4}$$

Step 3: If necessary, reduce the fraction to its simplest form.

$\frac{4}{5}$ cannot be reduced, and $\frac{2}{4} = \frac{1}{2}$.

To **add** or **subtract fractions** that have **different denominators,** first find the least common denominator (LCD).

Examples:

$$\frac{1}{2} + \frac{1}{6} = ? \text{ and } \frac{3}{4} - \frac{2}{3} = ?$$

Step 1: Write the equivalent fractions with a common denominator.

$$\frac{3}{6} + \frac{1}{6} = ? \text{ and } \frac{9}{12} - \frac{8}{12} = ?$$

Step 2: Add or subtract.

$$\frac{3}{6} + \frac{1}{6} = \frac{4}{6} \text{ and } \frac{9}{12} - \frac{8}{12} = \frac{1}{12}$$

Step 3: If necessary, reduce the fraction to its simplest form.

$\frac{4}{6} = \frac{2}{3}$, and $\frac{1}{12}$ cannot be reduced.

Multiplying Fractions

To **multiply fractions,** multiply the numerators and the denominators together, and then reduce the fraction to its simplest form.

Example:

$$\frac{5}{9} \times \frac{7}{10} = ?$$

Step 1: Multiply the numerators and denominators.

$$\frac{5}{9} \times \frac{7}{10} = \frac{5 \times 7}{9 \times 10} = \frac{35}{90}$$

Step 2: Reduce.

$$\frac{35}{90} = \frac{35 \div 5}{90 \div 5} = \frac{7}{18}$$

Dividing Fractions

To **divide fractions,** first rewrite the divisor (the number you divide *by*) upside down. This is called the reciprocal of the divisor. Then you can multiply and reduce if necessary.

Example:

$$\frac{5}{8} \div \frac{3}{2} = ?$$

Step 1: Rewrite the divisor as its reciprocal.

$$\frac{3}{2} \rightarrow \frac{2}{3}$$

Step 2: Multiply.

$$\frac{5}{8} \times \frac{2}{3} = \frac{5 \times 2}{8 \times 3} = \frac{10}{24}$$

Step 3: Reduce.

$$\frac{10}{24} = \frac{10 \div 2}{24 \div 2} = \frac{5}{12}$$

Scientific Notation

Scientific notation is a short way of representing very large and very small numbers without writing all of the place-holding zeros.

Example: Write 653,000,000 in scientific notation.

Step 1: Write the number without the place-holding zeros.

653

Step 2: Place the decimal point after the first digit.

6.53

Step 3: Find the exponent by counting the number of places that you moved the decimal point.

6.53000000

The decimal point was moved eight places to the left. Therefore, the exponent of 10 is positive 8. Remember, if the decimal point had moved to the right, the exponent would be negative.

Step 4: Write the number in scientific notation.

$$6.53 \times 10^8$$

Area

Area is the number of square units needed to cover the surface of an object.

Formulas:
Area of a square = side × side
Area of a rectangle = length × width
Area of a triangle = $\frac{1}{2}$ × base × height

Examples: Find the areas.

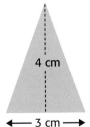

Triangle
Area = $\frac{1}{2}$ × base × height
Area = $\frac{1}{2}$ × 3 cm × 4 cm
Area = **6 cm²**

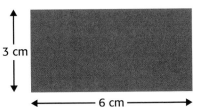

Rectangle
Area = length × width
Area = 6 cm × 3 cm
Area = **18 cm²**

Square
Area = side × side
Area = 3 cm × 3 cm
Area = **9 cm²**

Volume

Volume is the amount of space something occupies.

Formulas:
Volume of a cube = side × side × side

Volume of a prism = area of base × height

Examples:
Find the volume of the solids.

Cube
Volume = side × side × side
Volume = 4 cm × 4 cm × 4 cm
Volume = **64 cm³**

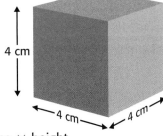

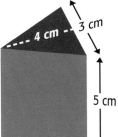

Prism
Volume = area of base × height
Volume = (area of triangle) × height
Volume = $\left(\frac{1}{2} \times 3 \text{ cm} \times 4 \text{ cm} \right)$ × 5 cm
Volume = 6 cm² × 5 cm
Volume = **30 cm³**

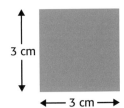

Periodic Table of the Elements

Each square on the table includes an element's name, chemical symbol, atomic number, and atomic mass.

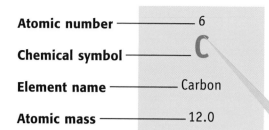

Atomic number ——— 6

Chemical symbol ——— C

Element name ——— Carbon

Atomic mass ——— 12.0

The background color indicates the type of element. Carbon is a nonmetal.

The color of the chemical symbol indicates the physical state at room temperature. Carbon is a solid.

Background
- Metals
- Metalloids
- Nonmetals

Chemical Symbol
- Solid
- Liquid
- Gas

Period 1

1
H
Hydrogen
1.0

	Group 1	Group 2		Group 3	Group 4	Group 5	Group 6	Group 7	Group 8	Group 9
Period 2	3 **Li** Lithium 6.9	4 **Be** Beryllium 9.0								
Period 3	11 **Na** Sodium 23.0	12 **Mg** Magnesium 24.3								
Period 4	19 **K** Potassium 39.1	20 **Ca** Calcium 40.1		21 **Sc** Scandium 45.0	22 **Ti** Titanium 47.9	23 **V** Vanadium 50.9	24 **Cr** Chromium 52.0	25 **Mn** Manganese 54.9	26 **Fe** Iron 55.8	27 **Co** Cobalt 58.9
Period 5	37 **Rb** Rubidium 85.5	38 **Sr** Strontium 87.6		39 **Y** Yttrium 88.9	40 **Zr** Zirconium 91.2	41 **Nb** Niobium 92.9	42 **Mo** Molybdenum 95.9	43 **Tc** Technetium (97.9)	44 **Ru** Ruthenium 101.1	45 **Rh** Rhodium 102.9
Period 6	55 **Cs** Cesium 132.9	56 **Ba** Barium 137.3		57 **La** Lanthanum 138.9	72 **Hf** Hafnium 178.5	73 **Ta** Tantalum 180.9	74 **W** Tungsten 183.8	75 **Re** Rhenium 186.2	76 **Os** Osmium 190.2	77 **Ir** Iridium 192.2
Period 7	87 **Fr** Francium (223.0)	88 **Ra** Radium (226.0)		89 **Ac** Actinium (227.0)	104 **Rf** Rutherfordium (261.1)	105 **Db** Dubnium (262.1)	106 **Sg** Seaborgium (263.1)	107 **Bh** Bohrium (262.1)	108 **Hs** Hassium (265)	109 **Mt** Meitnerium (266)

A row of elements is called a period.

A column of elements is called a group or family.

Lanthanides

58 **Ce** Cerium 140.1	59 **Pr** Praseodymium 140.9	60 **Nd** Neodymium 144.2	61 **Pm** Promethium (144.9)	62 **Sm** Samarium 150.4

Actinides

90 **Th** Thorium 232.0	91 **Pa** Protactinium 231.0	92 **U** Uranium 238.0	93 **Np** Neptunium (237.0)	94 **Pu** Plutonium 244.1

These elements are placed below the table to allow the table to be narrower.

This zigzag line reminds you where the metals, nonmetals, and metalloids are.

Group 18

| | 2 **He** Helium 4.0 |

Group 13 · **Group 14** · **Group 15** · **Group 16** · **Group 17**

| 5 **B** Boron 10.8 | 6 **C** Carbon 12.0 | 7 **N** Nitrogen 14.0 | 8 **O** Oxygen 16.0 | 9 **F** Fluorine 19.0 | 10 **Ne** Neon 20.2 |

| 13 **Al** Aluminum 27.0 | 14 **Si** Silicon 28.1 | 15 **P** Phosphorus 31.0 | 16 **S** Sulfur 32.1 | 17 **Cl** Chlorine 35.5 | 18 **Ar** Argon 39.9 |

Group 10 · **Group 11** · **Group 12**

| 28 **Ni** Nickel 58.7 | 29 **Cu** Copper 63.5 | 30 **Zn** Zinc 65.4 | 31 **Ga** Gallium 69.7 | 32 **Ge** Germanium 72.6 | 33 **As** Arsenic 74.9 | 34 **Se** Selenium 79.0 | 35 **Br** Bromine 79.9 | 36 **Kr** Krypton 83.8 |

| 46 **Pd** Palladium 106.4 | 47 **Ag** Silver 107.9 | 48 **Cd** Cadmium 112.4 | 49 **In** Indium 114.8 | 50 **Sn** Tin 118.7 | 51 **Sb** Antimony 121.8 | 52 **Te** Tellurium 127.6 | 53 **I** Iodine 126.9 | 54 **Xe** Xenon 131.3 |

| 78 **Pt** Platinum 195.1 | 79 **Au** Gold 197.0 | 80 **Hg** Mercury 200.6 | 81 **Tl** Thallium 204.4 | 82 **Pb** Lead 207.2 | 83 **Bi** Bismuth 209.0 | 84 **Po** Polonium (209.0) | 85 **At** Astatine (210.0) | 86 **Rn** Radon (222.0) |

| 110 **Uun*** Ununnilium (271) | 111 **Uuu*** Unununium (272) | 112 **Uub*** Ununbium (277) | | 114 **Uuq*** Ununquadium (285) | | 116 **Uuh*** Ununhexium (289) | | 118 **Uuo*** Ununoctium (293) |

A number in parenthesis is the mass number of the most stable form of that element.

| 63 **Eu** Europium 152.0 | 64 **Gd** Gadolinium 157.3 | 65 **Tb** Terbium 158.9 | 66 **Dy** Dysprosium 162.5 | 67 **Ho** Holmium 164.9 | 68 **Er** Erbium 167.3 | 69 **Tm** Thulium 168.9 | 70 **Yb** Ytterbium 173.0 | 71 **Lu** Lutetium 175.0 |

| 95 **Am** Americium (243.1) | 96 **Cm** Curium (247.1) | 97 **Bk** Berkelium (247.1) | 98 **Cf** Californium (251.1) | 99 **Es** Einsteinium (252.1) | 100 **Fm** Fermium (257.1) | 101 **Md** Mendelevium (258.1) | 102 **No** Nobelium (259.1) | 103 **Lr** Lawrencium (262.1) |

*The official names and symbols for the elements greater than 109 will eventually be approved by a committee of scientists.

Glossary

A

acid any compound that increases the number of hydrogen ions when dissolved in water and whose solution tastes sour and can change the color of certain compounds; acids turn blue litmus red, react with metals to produce hydrogen gas, and react with limestone or baking soda to produce carbon dioxide gas (57)

activation energy the minimum amount of energy needed for substances to react (40)

alpha particle a type of nuclear radiation consisting of two protons and two neutrons emitted by the nucleus of a radioactive atom; identical to the nucleus of a helium atom (81)

B

base any compound that increases the number of hydroxide ions when dissolved in water and whose solution tastes bitter, feels slippery, and can change the color of certain compounds; bases turn red litmus blue (59)

beta decay the release of a beta particle from a nucleus (82)

beta particle an electron or positron emitted by the nucleus of a radioactive atom (82)

biochemicals organic compounds made by living things (64)

C

carbohydrates biochemicals composed of one or more simple sugars bonded together that are used as a source of energy and for energy storage (64)

catalyst (KAT uh LIST) a substance that speeds up a reaction without being permanently changed (43)

chemical bond a force of attraction that holds two atoms together (4)

chemical bonding the joining of atoms to form new substances (4)

chemical equation a shorthand description of a chemical reaction using chemical formulas and symbols (32)

chemical formula a shorthand notation for a compound or a diatomic element using chemical symbols and numbers (30)

chemical reaction the process by which one or more substances undergo change to produce one or more different substances (28)

concentration a measure of the amount of solute dissolved in a solvent (42)

covalent (KOH VAY luhnt) **bond** the force of attraction between the nuclei of atoms and the electrons shared by the atoms (12)

covalent compounds compounds that are composed of elements that are covalently bonded; these compounds are composed of independent molecules, tend to have low melting and boiling points, do not usually dissolve in water, and form solutions that do not conduct an electric current when they do dissolve (55)

crystal lattice (LAT is) a repeating three-dimensional pattern of ions (11)

D

decomposition reaction a reaction in which a single compound breaks down to form two or more simpler substances (37)

double-replacement reaction a reaction in which ions in two compounds switch places (38)

ductility (duhk TIL uh tee) the ability of a substance to be drawn or pulled into a wire (16)

E

electrons the negatively charged particles found in all atoms; electrons are involved in the formation of chemical bonds (5, 16)

endothermic the term used to describe a physical or a chemical change in which energy is absorbed (40)

exothermic the term used to describe a physical or a chemical change in which energy is released or removed (39)

G

gamma decay the release of gamma rays from a nucleus (82)

gamma rays EM waves with very high energy and no mass or charge; they are emitted by the nucleus of a radioactive atom (82)

group a column of elements on the periodic table (6)

H

half-life the amount of time it takes for one-half of the nuclei of a radioactive isotope to decay (86)

halogens the elements in Group 17 of the periodic table; they are very reactive nonmetals, and their atoms have seven electrons in their outer level (17)

hydrocarbons organic compounds that are composed of only carbon and hydrogen (68)

I

inhibitor a substance that slows down or stops a chemical reaction (43)

ionic (ie AHN ik) **bond** the force of attraction between oppositely charged ions (8)

ionic compounds compounds that contain ionic bonds; composed of ions arranged in a crystal lattice, they tend to have high melting and boiling points, are solid at room temperature, and dissolve in water to form solutions that conduct an electric current (54)

ions charged particles that form during chemical changes when one or more valence electrons transfer from one atom to another (8)

isotopes atoms that have the same number of protons but have different numbers of neutrons (82, 85)

L

law of conservation of energy the law that states that energy is neither created nor destroyed (40)

law of conservation of mass the law that states that mass is neither created nor destroyed in ordinary chemical and physical changes (35)

lipids biochemicals that do not dissolve in water; their functions include storing energy and making up cell membranes; lipids include waxes, fats, and oils (65)

M

malleability (MAL ee uh BIL uh tee) the ability of a substance to be pounded into thin sheets (16)

mass number the sum of the protons and neutrons in an atom (81)

metallic bond the force of attraction between a positively charged metal ion and the electrons in a metal (15)

molecule (MAHL i KYOOL) a neutral group of atoms held together by covalent bonds (12)

N

noble gases the unreactive elements in Group 18 of the periodic table; their atoms have eight electrons in their outer level (except for helium, which has two electrons) (6)

nuclear (NOO klee uhr) **chain reaction** a continuous series of nuclear fission reactions (89)

nuclear energy the form of energy associated with changes in the nucleus of an atom (88, 92)

nuclear fission the process in which a large nucleus splits into two smaller nuclei (88, 89)

nuclear fusion the process in which two or more nuclei with small masses join together, or fuse, to form a larger, more massive nucleus (92)

nuclear radiation high-energy particles and rays that are emitted by the nuclei of some atoms; alpha particles, beta particles, and gamma rays are types of nuclear radiation (80)

nucleic acids biochemicals that store information and help to build proteins and other nucleic acids; made up of subunits called nucleotides (67)

nucleus (NOO klee uhs) the tiny, extremely dense, positively charged region in the center of an atom; made up of protons and neutrons (84, 85)

O

organic compounds covalent compounds composed of carbon-based molecules (63)

P

pH a measure of hydronium ion concentration in a solution; a pH of 7 is neutral; a pH less than 7 is acidic; a pH greater than 7 is basic (60)

plasma the state of matter that does not have a definite shape or volume and whose particles have broken apart; plasma is composed of electrons and positively charged ions (92)

positron a beta particle with a charge of 1+ and a mass of almost 0 (82)

products the substances formed from a chemical reaction (32)

proteins biochemicals that are composed of amino acids; their functions include regulating chemical activities, transporting and storing materials, and providing structural support (66)

protons the positively charged particles of the nucleus; the number of protons in a nucleus is the atomic number that determines the identity of an element (84–85)

R

radioactive decay the process in which the nucleus of a radioactive atom releases nuclear radiation (81)

radioactivity the ability of some elements to give off nuclear radiation (80)

reactants (ree AK TUHNTS) the starting materials in a chemical reaction (32)

S

salt an ionic compound formed from the positive ion of a base and the negative ion of an acid (62)

saturated hydrocarbon a hydrocarbon in which each carbon atom in the molecule shares a single bond with each of four other atoms; an alkane (68)

scientific method a series of steps that scientists use to answer questions and solve problems (116)

single-replacement reaction a reaction in which an element takes the place of another element in a compound; this can occur only when a more-reactive element takes the place of a less-reactive one (37)

solubility (SAHL yoo BIL uh tee) the ability to dissolve in another substance; more specifically, the amount of solute needed to make a saturated solution using a given amount of solvent at a certain temperature (55–56)

subscript a number written below and to the right of a chemical symbol in a chemical formula (30)

synthesis (SIN thuh sis) **reaction** a reaction in which two or more substances combine to form a single compound (36)

T

theory a unifying explanation for a broad range of hypotheses and observations that have been supported by testing (4)

tracer a radioactive element whose path can be followed through a process or reaction (87)

U

unsaturated hydrocarbon a hydrocarbon in which at least two carbon atoms share a double bond (an alkene) or a triple bond (an alkyne) (68)

V

valence (VAY luhns) **electrons** the electrons in the outermost energy level of an atom; these electrons are involved in forming chemical bonds (5)

Index

Credits

Abbreviations used: (t) top, (c) center, (b) bottom, (l) left, (r) right, (bkgd) background

ILLUSTRATIONS

All illustrations, unless noted below, by Holt, Rinehart and Winston.

Chapter One Page 5, Stephen Durke/Washington Artists; 6, Preface, Inc.; 7, 9, 10, Stephen Durke/Washington Artists; 11(t), Keith Locke/Suzanne Craig; 11(br), Kristy Sprott; 12(c), 13(tl), Stephen Durke/Washington Artists; 13(tr,c), Preface, Inc.; 14(tr,br), Kristy Sprott; 14(bl), Stephen Durke/Washington Artists; 15, Kristy Sprott; 16(cl), 17(tc), Kristy Sprott; 17(br), Preface, Inc.; 20(t), Keith Locke/Suzanne Craig; 20(b), Stephen Durke/Washington Artists; 21, Kristy Sprott; 22(b), Stephen Durke/Washington Artists; 24, Kristy Sprott.

Chapter Two Page 30(t), 34, Kristy Sprott; 36(b), 37(c,b), 38(b), Blake Thornton/Rita Marie; 41(t), 43(b), Preface, Inc.; 46, Blake Thornton/Rita Marie; 47, Kristy Sprott; 49(cr), Preface, Inc.;

Chapter Three Page 60(t), Dave Joly; 60(b), 63, Preface, Inc.; 64, 65(b), Morgan Cain & Associates; 68, 69(b), 75(tr), Preface, Inc.

Chapter Four Page 81, 82, Stephen Durke/Washington Artists; 83, Gary Ferster; 84, 85, Stephen Durke/Washington Artists; 86, Preface, Inc.; 88, 89, Stephen Durke/Washington Artists; 90, Patrick Gnan/Deborah Wolfe Ltd.; 92(c), 96(br), 98, Stephen Durke/Washington Artists; 99(tr), Preface, Inc.

Appendix Page 114(t), Terry Guyer; 118(b), Mark Mille/Sharon Langley Artist Rep.; 119, 120, 121, Preface, Inc.; 126, 127, Kristy Sprott.

PHOTOGRAPHY

Cover and Title page: Tom Pantages

Table of Contents p. v(t), Richard Megna Fundamental Photographs; v(b), Dennis Kunkel/University of Hawaii; vi(t), Tom Stewart/The Stock Market; vi(c), Richard Haynes/HRW Photo; vi(b), Hans Reinhard/Bruce Coleman, Inc.; vii, Richard Megna Fundamental Photographs.

Feature Borders Unless otherwise noted below, all images ©2001 PhotoDisc/HRW: "Across the Sciences" 24, 76, all images by HRW; "Careers" 51, 101, sand bkgd and saturn, Corbis Images, DNA, Morgan Cain & Associates, scuba gear, ©1997 Radlund & Associates for Artville; "Eureka" 25, ©2001 PhotoDisc/HRW; "Eye on the Environment" 50, clouds and sea in bkgd, HRW, bkgd grass and red eyed frog, Corbis Images, hawks and pelican, Animals Animals/Earth Scenes, rat, John Grelach/Visuals Unlimited, endangered flower, Dan Suzio/Photo Researchers, Inc.; "Scientific Debate" 100, Sam Dudgeon/HRW Photo; "Weird Science" 77, mite, David Burder/Stone, atom balls, J/B Woolsey Associates, walking stick and turtle, EclectiCollection.

Chapter One pp. 2-3 Douglas Struthers/Stone; 3 HRW Photo; 8(t), Kevin Schafer/Peter Arnold, Inc.; 8(l), Peter Van Steen/HRW Photo; 11(l), Paul Silverman/Fundamental Photographs; 15(r), Calder Sculpture, National Museum in Washington D.C. Photo © Ted Mahiec/The Stock Market; 16 Victoria Smith/HRW Photo; 22, Victoria Smith/HRW Photo.

Chapter Two pp. 26-27 Nicholas Pinturas/Stone; 27 HRW Photo; 28(t), Rob Matheson/The Stock Market; 28(br), Dorling Kindersley, LTD.; 29(tl), Charles D. Winters/Timeframe Photography Inc.; 29(tr), Richard Megna/Fundamental Photographs; 29(br), Dr. E.R. Degginger/Color-Pic, Inc.; 32(b), Richard Haynes/ HRW Photo; 33(r), Charles D. Winters/Photo Researchers, Inc.; 33(l), Mark C. Burnett/Photo Researchers, Inc.; 35(l,r), Michael Dalton/Fundamental Photographs; 36, Richard Megna/Fundamental Photographs; 37, Charles D. Winters/Photo Researchers, Inc.; 38(l), Peticolas/Megna/Fundamental Photographs; 38(r), Richard Megna/Fundamental Photographs; 39(c), Peter Van Steen/HRW Photo; 39(r), Tom Stewart/The Stock Market; 39(l), Victoria Smith/HRW Photo; 42(t, bl, br), Richard Megna/Fundamental Photographs; 43, Dorling Kindersley, LTD, courtesy of the Science Museum, London; 48(t), 49, Richard Megna/Fundamental Photographs. 50, John Deeks/Photo Researchers, Inc.; 51 (tl,br), Bob Parker/Austin Fire Investigation.

Chapter Three pp. 52-53 W. Gladstone/Great Barrier Reef marine Park Authority; 53 HRW Photo; 54(t), Yoav Levy/Phototake; 55(t, bl, br), 56, Richard Megna/Fundamental Photographs; 57(b), Charles D. Winters/Timeframe Photography Inc.; 61(t), Runk/Schoenberger/Grant Heilman Photography Inc.; 61(b), Peter Arnold Inc., NY; 62, Miro Vinton/Stock Boston/PNI; 66(br), Hans Reinhard/Bruce Coleman Inc.; 67, David M. Phillips/ Visuals Unlimited; 68(br), Charles D. Winters/Timeframe Photography Inc.; 72, Runk Schoenberger/Grant Heilman Photography; 74(b), Charles D. Winters/Timeframe Photography Inc.; 74(t), Richard Megna/Fundamental Photographs; 76, Sygma; 77(t), Tom McHugh/Photo Researchers, Inc.; 77(b), Dennis Kunkel, University of Hawaii.

Chapter Four pp. 78-79 GJLP/CNRI/Phototake; 79 HRW Photo; 80(b), Henri Becquerel/The Granger Collection; 80(t), Dr. E.R. Degginger/Color-Pic, Inc.; 85, Sygma; 87(b), Tim Wright/Corbis; 87(t), Custom Medical Stock Photo; 89, Emory Kristof/National Geographic Image Collection; 91(t), Shone/Liaison International; 91(b), Michael Melford/The Image Bank; 92, Roger Rossmeyer/Corbis Bettmann; 96, Dr. E.R. Degginger/Color-Pic, Inc.; 97, Emory Kristof/National Geographic Image Collection; 99(r), Science Photo Library/Photo Researchers, Inc.; 100(b), Sauder/Gamma Liason; 100(t), Cameramann International; 101(t), Courtesy of Micheal Atzmon.; 101(b), Charles O'Rear/Corbis Images.

LabBook "LabBook Header": "L," Corbis Images, "a," Letraset Phototone, "b" and "B," HRW, "o" and "k," images ©2001 PhotoDisc/HRW; 103(c), Michelle Bridwell/HRW Photo; 103(br), Image copyright © 2001 PhotoDisc, Inc.; 104(cl), Victoria Smith/HRW Photo; 104(bl), Stephanie Morris/HRW Photo; 105(tr), Jana Birchum/HRW Photo; 105(b), Peter Van Steen/HRW Photo; 109-110, Victoria Smith/HRW Photo.

Appendix p. 115(b), Sam Dudgeon/HRW Photo; 115(t), Peter Van Steen/HRW Photo.

Sam Dudgeon/HRW Photo p. vii-1, 14; 15(l); 19; 23; 25; 28(bl); 34; 45; 54(b); 58(b); 66(bl); 68(t); 70; 75; 90; 93; 94; 95; 102; 103(b); 105(tl); 106; 107; 104(br, t).

John Langford/HRW Photo p. 4; 8(r); 12; 17; 32(t); 33(c); 40-41; 48(b); 57(t); 58(b); 59; 68(bl); 69; 99(l); 103(t); 111.

Scott Van Osdol/HRW Photo p. 29(bl); 64; 65; 66(t); 73.

Self-Check Answers

Chapter 1—Chemical Bonding

Page 9: neon

Page 13: 1. 6 **2.** In a covalent bond, electrons are shared between atoms. In an ionic bond, electrons are transferred from one atom to another.

Chapter 2—Chemical Reactions

Page 31: 2 sodium atoms, 1 sulfur atom, and 4 oxygen atoms

Page 33: $CaBr_2 + Cl_2 \rightarrow Br_2 + CaCl_2$

reactants: $CaBr_2$ and Cl_2

products: Br_2 and $CaCl_2$

Chapter 3—Chemical Compounds

Page 61: a soft drink

Chapter 4—Atomic Energy

Page 82: alpha particles